M000113376

Mark Leigh gained his super powers after crash-landing on Earth as a baby to escape the destruction of his home planet. However, although not able to fly or leap tall buildings, Mark has the uncanny ability to find the slowest moving queue, get stuck behind the only driver wanting to turn right and leave the house with his flies open.
Mark is twentysomething and lives in Wimbledon with his wife Debbie and baby daughter, Polly. He wants loads of people to buy this book so that he can afford to buy Polly a pony, ballet lessons and all that other stuff that little girls want.

Mike Lepine gained his uncanny comedic writing powers after accidental exposure to a potentially cataclysmic combination of Woody Allen, Monty Python, Jack Daniels and Glen Fiddich. Now, by day he is a mild-mannered advertising account manager but, by night, he becomes one with his trusty Amstrad PCW8256 and sets out on his sworn mission to expose injustice, slam hypocrisy and earn some very handy spare cash into the bargain.
Mike lives with girlfriend, Philippa, and golden retriever puppy, Raglan, in Harrow, Middlesex. His ambition is to live somewhere else.

In 1978 sixteen-year-old Steve Dillon was bitten by a radioactive bed-bug which gave him the power to out-sleep the average hibernating grizzly bear. This caused more than a few problems as he was just starting out as a full-time, professional comic artist with Marvel UK and 2000 AD. A burst of energy followed that allowed him to co-create Deadline magazine in 1988. After moving to Dublin in 1989, however, Steve was struck by lightning and became capable of staying immersed in a vat of Guinness for days on end, getting out only to buy the occasional packet of dry-roast peanuts.
Steve is currently drawing Animal Man for DC comics.

Other books by Mark Leigh and Mike Lepine:

The Complete Revenge Kit, How To Be A Complete Bastard (with Adrian Edmondson), How To Be A Complete Bitch (with Pamela Stephenson), The Book Of Revelations, The Naughty 90s, The Return Of The Complete Revenge Kit

ISBN 1-56163-051-9
©Mark Leigh and Mike Lepine 1992
Illustrations©Steve Dillon 1992
Cover©David Horsey 1992

1 2 3 4 5 6 7 8 9

Send for our complete catalog of
graphic novels:
NBM
185 Madison Ave., Ste. 1502
New York, NY 10016

HOW TO BE A

Mark Leigh
Mike Lepine
Illustrated by
Steve Dillon

NANTIER · BEALL · MINOUSTCHINE
Publishing inc.
new york

With special thanks to our *super* friends:

Alisdair Alexander, John Choopani, Rob Ewen, Philippa Hatton, Gill and Neville Landau, Debbie Leigh, Gaye and Fred Leonard, Ravi Mirchandani, Chris Phillips, Lino Raffia, Mandy and Peter Speck, Tracy Wheeler

... Continued from page 114.

SO PICK YOU UP AROUND 8.30 ON TUESDAY, OKAY?

SOUNDS GREAT! LOOKING FORWARD TO IT! TAKE CARE, MAN!

YEAH, YOU TOO!

TO THE PURCHASER:
Guarantee: If you fail to save the Universe, and it is subsequently destroyed, you may claim back the full purchase price of this book at any surviving stockist on presentation of receipt. Failure to save a parallel and/or anti-matter universe are not grounds for reimbursement.

TO THE RETAILER:
You may accept this book back for refund, should the Universe as we know it cease to exist. The publisher will reimburse you in full for the transaction, plus usual handling charge. Void where prohibited by law. Offer ends 31 December 3117.

HOW TO USE THIS BOOK

SUPER POWERS AND SECRET ORIGINS

SPELL IT OUT FOR ME, GUYS. WHAT *IS* A SUPERHERO?

THE SUPERHERO'S FIRST EASY PRIMER

THIS IS A SUPERHERO

THIS IS A SUPERVILLAIN

THE SUPERHERO BEATS THE LIVING CRAP OUT OF THE SUPERVILLAIN

THE UNIVERSE IS SAFE AGAIN!

There, in essence, we have it. A superhero is someone who (quote) 'beats the living crap out of a supervillain'. Sounds appealing?

If this is what you'd like to do with your life, then your super-career starts here!

WHY SHOULD I BECOME A SUPERHERO?

Beating the living crap out of supervillains can be rewarding work in itself, but never forget that being a superhero is just plain, good old-fashioned fun as well!

After all, in what other profession can you run around in a cape, jump off buildings, swing on flagpoles or run down Main Street screaming 'Show yourself, Invisible Lashlord!' and not get dragged away by the police on suspicion of a major drugs violation?

SOUNDS GREAT! BUT IS THERE ANYTHING YOU'RE NOT TELLING ME?

There are, of course, some potential drawbacks too, like sudden violent death, being marooned on Neptune or turning into a rampaging swamp beast by mistake ... but true superheroes find this kind of danger an added turn-on!

We asked a selection of world-famous superheroes what they thought the single biggest drawback of being a superhero was...

SUPERHEROES SPEAK !

'Going out when it's raining!'
— *Mightyman, New York, NY*

'Working nights...'
— *Moonwarrior, Norfolk, VA*

'Wearing tights in public...'
— *Captain Republican, Waco, TX*

'Having to save the world on weekends, when everyone else is at the beach!'
— *The Hooded Arrow, Atlantic City, NJ*

'Not being able to adequately control my powers! Every time I looked at my wife and got aroused, I'd spontaneously ignite to a surface temperature of 87,000° C. We're having a trial separation now. She's hiding somewhere in Nepal...'
— *Inferno, San Bernadino, CA*

'Flying off to Neptune at a moment's notice ... Neptune sucks worse than Detroit'
— *Mr Cosmic, Des Moines, IA*

'Having to risk your life to save places you don't particularly like'
— *Firefight, Cleveland, OH*

'Having people whisper among themselves when you and your Boy Wonder hit the street'
— *Captain Butch, Sacramento, CA*

ER, WHAT WAS THAT YOU MENTIONED EARLIER ABOUT BECOMING A RAMPAGING SWAMP BEAST BY ACCIDENT! HOW CAN I AVOID THIS?

That's simple! When you're attempting to become a superhero, don't do it in a swamp! For that matter, don't even get too close to a compost heap, a bag of mulch, Cleveland Ohio or a Turkish restaurant when you make your bid for powers!

If you ignore this advice, you will invariably be turned into a rampaging swamp beast – which is something you don't want to be.

Although, technically, many rampaging swamp beasts are classified as superheroes, generally speaking they have a rough time of it. They're not allowed in many bars and restaurants, they can't use public swimming pools (because they'll turn the water murky) and if, in their private lives, they ever succeed in disguising their true brackish nature and find employment, they're usually passed over for promotion in favor of someone who doesn't stink or have tree roots protruding out of his ass.

Furthermore, no rampaging swamp beast has ever won a Nobel Prize, become President or got even to first base with either Stevie Nicks or Tiffany (Madonna is another matter).

But probably the biggest drawback of all is trying to maintain a secret civilian identity. Rampaging swamp beasts are notoriously conspicious, even in a decent suit, and may have to continually humiliate themselves in an effort to conceal their true nature and hence face instant dismissal...

THE BOSS: Ah, come in, Mr Everglades. I've been wanting to see you!

MR EVERGLADES: Oh? What about, sir?

THE BOSS: Yeah ... right ... well, where to begin? Your face for a start, I guess...

MR EVERGLADES: Yes?

THE BOSS: Well, it's covered in mud.

MR EVERGLADES: It's a mudpack, sir. I have eczema and my doctor recommended it for me.

THE BOSS: I see ... You're awfully big as well, aren't you?

MR EVERGLADES: Healthy living, sir. Lots of fibre!

THE BOSS: Hmmm! Nine feet tall ... There's no easy way to say this, Mr Everglades, so I'm going to come straight out with it. You're not a ... how can I say this ... a *rampaging swamp beast*, are you? Because you know our company policy regarding employing rampaging swamp beasts...

MR EVERGLADES: No, sir!

THE BOSS: Only you ... um ... you smell like one...

MR EVERGLADES: Oh, that ... ah ... I just had an accident in my pants, that's all sir! Ha ha! Ha!

THE BOSS: Oh. Do you ... often have such ... accidents?

MR EVERGLADES: Oh yes! All the time, sir! '*Mr Sh..-His-Pants*' that's what they call me down in the mail room! Ha! Ha!

THE BOSS: And you have tropical fruits growing out of your ear!

MR EVERGLADES: Ah ... that's my hobby, sir!

THE BOSS: What?

MR EVERGLADES: Tropical fruit growing ... in my ears, sir! Very rewarding!

THE BOSS: Oh ... Jesus ... I must open a window in here! Look, Mr Everglades, there's other things too. For a start, you leave a trail of slime.

MR EVERGLADES: So does Mr Seligman, sir!

THE BOSS: That's different. He's the company accountant. You expect that. And then there's the matter of your lunchbox. How long have you been eating decaying vegetation rolls, Mr Everglades?

MR EVERGLADES: They're macrobiotic, sir. Very healthy. My wife makes them for me.

THE BOSS: Yes ... your wife. I met her at the last Christmas party ... Are you aware that your wife ... is an alligator, Mr Everglades?

MR EVERGLADES: Is she?

THE BOSS: Oh, yes.

MR EVERGLADES: That's funny. I never noticed that.

THE BOSS: You're not a very close couple then.

MR EVERGLADES: We're both busy pursuing different careers, sir. We don't have much time to spend together.

THE BOSS: I don't buy it! I'd notice if my wife was an alligator, and I put more hours into this company than anyone else! I put it to you, Mr Everglades, that you are indeed a rampaging swamp beast and that you obtained your job here by deception! Now get out!

MR EVERGLADES: Yes ... sir ...

THE BOSS. Oh, and on your way out tell Mr Bayou and Ms Mangrove that I'd like a word with them in my office too...

I'VE READ THAT YOU CAN GET SUPERPOWERS BY HITTING YOURSELF ABOUT THE HEAD WITH A MALLET. IS THIS TRUE?

No.

I'VE ALSO HEARD THAT I CAN SELL MY SOUL TO THE DEVIL IN EXCHANGE FOR POWERS. SHOULD I CONSIDER THIS OPTION?

Again, no. Many superheroes try this, hoping to renege on the contract at a later date. What they don't realize is that the contract they have just signed is the most airtight in the Universe. After all, where do you think lawyers go when they die?

HOW ELSE SHOULD I AVOID GETTING MY SUPER POWERS?

➡ Never buy superpowers by mail order
➡ Never trust anyone who says they can give you superpowers by rubbing your groin (unless it's a pretty girl: then you can humor her)
➡ Never trust anyone selling superpowers from door to door
➡ Never trust anyone selling superpowers in a bar – they're either stolen or damaged

If you believed all those dumb comic book covers in the 1960s and your motive for gaining superpowers is to impress girls, forget it!

In reality, the girlfriends of superheroes invariably get killed/ despise your alter ego/turn into a Marauding Rock Monster/get held hostage by The Purple Demon/turn out to be mentally disturbed Ninja warrior women ... or, strangest of all seem to lose about thirty points off their IQ because they're unable to recognize you when you're wearing even the skimpiest of masks.

HOW CAN I OBTAIN SUPERPOWERS OF MY VERY OWN?

There are many ways to obtain superpowers, but *be warned*: the path is fraught with quite incredible danger and the odds are hugely in favor of you ending up horribly, horrendously and disabilitatingly injured, vaporized or spread unevenly across at least five states of the Union (which do not necessarily border each other) rather than as a superhero.

Didn't it warn you clearly on the blurb that enticed you to buy this book? Oh. Those little geeks publishers keep in broom cupboards especially to write these blurbs never, ever read the book first ... Sorry about that.

Anyway, here are some methods you might like to try – strictly at your own risk, of course.

BEING BORN WITH MUTANT SUPERPOWERS

This is, of course, the easiest method of obtaining superpowers. You may well, at this very moment, be a mutant with colossal powers of which you are not aware!

Think carefully: have you ever lifted up an eighteen-wheeler by mistake, punched your way through twelve inches of reinforced concrete by accident or flown to Neptune instead of going to school? If you have answered *yes* to any one of these, you may well have been born with mutant superpowers!

Alternatively, you could just be clinically insane, which is, unhappily, far more likely.

But even if your answer is no, don't despair! Many people have *latent* superpowers which are only revealed to them in moments of great stress or personal danger!

To discover whether or not you have latent mutant superpowers, try one or more of the following tests.

A) Stand directly in the path of an oncoming express train and see if your body transforms into titanium steel to absorb the impact.

B) Eat at a cheap Mexican restaurant to learn the extent of your invulnerability.

C) Wander into the girls' locker room at school and see if your latent power of invisibility can save you from expulsion and your parents from having to move out of the neighborhood in shame.

D) If that doesn't work, try jumping off the Empire State Building to see if your latent powers of flight will be forced to save you. (N.B. This is not a good way to learn that your latent power is invisibility after all.)

E) Finally, if all else fails, try wandering through the South Bronx at 2 a.m. dragging a transparent sack full of $20 bills, yelling out, 'Oh! I must hurry home with all my lovely lottery winnings!' and see if any kind of power on Earth can save you.

BEING EXPOSED TO RADIATION

Once all the rage in the 1950s and '60s, medical research has now shown that direct exposure to radiation is not a particularly good way to gain superpowers.

If you won't take our word for it, just ask the superheroes who have used this method in the past – Captain Leukemia, The Meltdown Man, Mr Low Sperm Count, Ms Low Sperm Count, The Inside-Out Man, The Incredible Cancer Victim or The Portentous Blotch.

If you're still determined to gain your powers in this fashion, just go and spend a few days within a hundred miles downwind of any nuclear power plant or processing factory.

DEVELOPING A NEW, SECRET FORMULA

While this didn't work for Coca-Cola, there's no reason to believe this won't work for you!

The trick is to concoct what *you* think is just the right combination of chemicals and then either drink them or tip them over your head to see what happens. (Throwing up or suddenly becoming a redhead are not sudden manifestations of superpowers. It's more likely that you've accidentally chemically recreated henna or Miller Lite.)

Of some two hundred people who have attempted this method, one gained superspeed, another the power to rotate his buttocks during the late spring and a third to scream louder and longer than any human being ever recorded. The others are all dead, resemble Silly Putty (in body, thought AND deed) or are currently exhausting their medical insurance – so it's far from an exact science, as you can see.

N.B. You might be forgiven for thinking it a good idea to try out your untested formula first, before using it yourself ... but experience seems to indicate otherwise...

BECOMING A HUMAN TORCH

Good Ways to Become a Human Torch:

➡ Vibrating every molecule of your body at superspeed until friction ignites your body at a cellular level

➡ Being bombarded by cosmic rays that interact with your body chemistry

➡ Learning the mysteries of an ancient race of volcano dwellers

➡ Getting bitten by a radioactive firefly

➡ Having a mother and father who are both Human Torches

Bad Ways to Become a Human Torch:

➡ Vibrating every molecule of your body at superspeed until it falls to bits

➡ Dowsing yourself in kerosene and striking a match

➡ Falling asleep while smoking in bed

➡ Volunteering for the Pentagon's napalm-testing program

➡ Making a Pepsi-Cola commercial

➡ Freebasing

JOINING THE INTERGALACTIC SPACE POLICE

The Intergalactic Space Police imbue all their Star Cops with Cosmic Superpowers to keep the peace throughout the known Universe – or at least in the sectors of the Galaxy where the rich and influential beings dwell.

The trouble is, you have to be selected rather than just joining up. The Intergalactic Space Police don't take just anyone! However, you can be sure that, like terrestrial police forces the world over, they're looking for certain character traits in their recruits, namely:

A) Below-average intelligence
B) Hatred for anyone different to themselves
C) A predilection for sticking the boot in (when no one's looking)

If you behave sufficiently badly, an alien emissary from the Space Police will contact you. If you instantly assault him or try to blow his brains out for being a 'vile tentacled reptile-faced asswipe from beyond space' – you're in! Offer to take him to your leader or behave in any friendly way whatsoever – and you automatically fail the test!

But BE WARNED: it's not easy being an Integalactic Space Cop, for a number of reasons...

1. How can you prevent crimes you don't even understand?
2. It's difficult to arrest beings who exist on wavelengths beyond the human visible range.
3. There are over two billion different types of felony and misdemeanor in the galaxy ... and you'll be expected to memorize the code for every single one...

2,004,671	Offenses against garden furniture by reptilian lifeforms
2,004,672	B&E involving sentient raspberries
2,004,673	Xammalanning off-world without permission in triplicate
2,004,674	Offenses against reptilian lifeforms by sentient garden furniture (retaliatory)
2,004,675	Action in breach of Rigellian Peace Convention involving use of a garden swing
2,004,676	Unicellular division in a public place
2,004,677	Drunk and disorderly (mature sentient yeasts excepted)
2,004,678	Niffling (with or without cornflakes).

Yes, it can be quite difficult and unpleasant being a Superhero in the Intergalactic Space Police...

BEING THE OFFSPRING OF A HUMAN FATHER AND AN ATLANTEAN MOTHER

Many people never discover that, because of their strange mixed parentage, they are blessed with prodigious aquatic superpowers. Ask yourself: could your mother really be a disguised mermaid?

Think long and hard about this...

➡ Does she ever have strands of seaweed protruding from the back of her blouse?

➡ Does she spend an *awful* long time in the bathroom?

➡ Does she take her legs off at night?

➡ Has she ever looked at a herring and said, 'Hello, Frank'?

➡ Does she side with the shark in *Jaws*?

➡ Does she ever look wistfully at dishwater?

➡ Have you ever caught a glimpse of her in a Jacques Cousteau film?

➡ Has she got mental control over turbot or any other seawater fish?

➡ Has she got an Atlantean passport?

➡ Has she ever packed raw seal chunks in your lunch box by mistake?

➡ Is she blue?

GETTING STRUCK BY LIGHTNING

Lightning is an awesome elemental force of nature, and its properties are still not fully understood. For example, many people now believe that lightning was responsible for starting life on Earth (but then, many people also believed Bush's campaign promises, so this doesn't mean too much by itself).

Whatever the secret of lightning, it is a potent force of nature and hence a great potential source of superpowers!

Good ways to be struck by lightning:

➡ Play golf in the midst of a ferocious thunderstorm – while sitting on your caddy's shoulders

➡ Stand on the observation deck of the Empire State Building with an eighty-foot lightning conductor strapped to your back (if you can fit in the elevator)

➡ Perform an ancient Hopi rain dance while wing-walking on a 747

➡ Skydive through a thunderstorm wearing a jump suit made entirely of aluminum foil

➡ Shout out rude things about God

➡ Shout out rude things about Billy Graham

➡ Fly a kite made of aluminum foil in the heart of a storm. Moor the kite strings to your head for maximum effect

➡ Pretend you're a very tall building

➡ Never go anywhere that lightning has struck before

➡ Play with yourself. (Well, that's what our parents always told us...)

VIGOROUS MASTURBATION

This method obviously doesn't work; Dan Quayle has no superpowers.

BEING BITTEN BY A RADIOACTIVE ANIMAL

Currently, the best places to find radioactive animals, if you want to be bitten by one, is anywhere downwind of the Chernobyl power plant – like northern Sweden or Lapland.

The animals living there are not the most exciting in the world to be bitten by, and will probably require a good deal of provocation or tugging about the scrotum before endowing you with your powers. In this instance, think very carefully: do you really want to be Captain Reindeer or The Incredible Elk? And what good are 'Uncanny Antler Powers' anyway?

It's best to choose the animal *you* want to bite you – and *then* contaminate it with the kind of nuclear waste you can find lying around any nuclear plant or factory. Choose carefully: The kind of animal you select will determine the kind of superpowers you receive...

Radioactive Dog

Will give you a super-enhanced sense of smell, which is great for tracking supervillains, but means that you can't live anywhere within 600 miles of New Jersey.

Radioactive Cat

Will give you amazing agility and probably some kind of 'nine lives' power, but also the urge to constantly mark your area of patrol with urine and unnaccountably run in front of oncoming traffic.

Radioactive Beaver

Superb when the opportunity arises to save the world by creating a giant log dam, but as The Beaver, will you be able to stand all the jibes from supervillains, like 'Yo! Beaver! Prepare for a lickin'!'?

It's not funny when you hear it for the hundreth time! (It's not so hot the first time either...). Pick another animal – and preferably not a cockerel or an ass.

Radioactive Spider

Sailing dangerously close to infringing several major copyrights. Steer clear.

Radioactive Halibut

Halibut have no teeth, so the question is academic.

Radioactive Diplodocus

If you can find one of these to bite you, good luck.

Radioactive Man-Eating Tiger

Will completely devour you.

Radioactive Sloth

Superb hanging-upside-down powers, but very little sense of urgency to combat injustice.

Radioactive Tuna

See Radioactive Halibut.

Radioactive Chameleon

Ability to blend in with your background and change color – especially useful when your patrol area encompasses several different New York neighborhoods.

Radioactive Owl

The ability to swivel your head through 360° can be quite disconcerting to a supervillain, especially if he's just seen *The Exorcist*. Superb powers for night crimefighting, but a silly battle cry ('Terwit-Terwoo').

Radioactive Leech

Instant qualification to practice law, accountancy or dentistry.

Radioactive Dolphin

For the superhero bent on thwarting crime beneath the waves, there is no substitute for being bitten by a radioactive dolphin! However, dolphins are notoriously reluctant to bite people – even the Japanese, who sorely deserve it – and may need some tricking or provoking. Try disguising yourself as an extra-large crunchy herring. Alternatively, try insulting the dolphin's intelligence by saying things like, 'Humans are the most intelligent species on the planet', 'We only ever dump toxins in the oceans by mistake' or 'Hello, Flipper'...

Radioactive Cheese

This is not an animal; it's a dairy product.

Radioactive Vulture

The power of flight – but you'll only ever show up after the battle is all over.

Radioactive Skunk

Believe us when we say you don't want to do this.

Radioactive Pufferfish

Alright, Pufferfish have no teeth, but they do have an exceptionally useful power, so fit yours with dentures. After being bitten, you will get the power to swell up to an enormous size whenever threatened, causing the supervillain to mistake you for Roseanne Barr and ask for your autograph instead of letting you have it with his Thermotron Ray Beam gun.

Radioactive Millipede

With so many pairs of legs, you will be able to race to the scene of the crime! Hiding your super-identity from your loved ones, however, is another matter and may necessitate you only ever being seen from the waist up. Try standing behind items of furniture during evenings and on weekends.

Radioactive Bandicoot

Fo#$ knows.

BEING BEQUEATHED YOUR POWERS BY A *BEING OF INFINITE WISDOM*

An excellent method! People are always being bequeathed superpowers by wizened old men who are really Beings of Infinite Wisdom and you could be next ... if you just know where to find them!

Paradoxically, no Being of Infinite Wisdom ever hangs out in the obvious places you'd expect anyone with some smarts to choose – like on the beach at Acapulco or in the Dallas Cowboy Cheerleaders' locker room – so it's no use looking there (sorry).

Instead, these Beings choose to live in far more unlikely places. We don't mean that they hang out at 'New Kids on the Block' concerts or ride the subway after dark (where you're much more likely to find Beings of Infinite Stupidity) or anything so drastic, but Beings of Infinite Wisdom have a predilection for draughty caves half way up K2, temples at the bottom of perilous gorges or 'Forbidden Cities' which haven't seen any improvement in sanitation or plumbing technology in over 2,000 years.

Go figure it...

Anyway, you will be able to tell a Being of Infinite Wisdom when you meet him in the following ways.

A) He will know your name and tell you he's been waiting for you
B) He won't have any novels by Jackie Collins on his bookshelf
C) He will usually be called something like 'The Ancient One' or 'The Venerated Master Who Sees All' (Any Beings of Infinite Wisdom you come across called 'Biff' or 'Sonny' are probably impostors)
D) He won't be able to skateboard or Moonwalk
E) If you ask him for a cigarette, he'll tell you he doesn't smoke
F) He won't know who J.R. Ewing is

Simply tell him that you've come seeking the power to combat injustice and deprivation (or that 'Greg' sent you – either works), and the superpowers you desire will be yours!

SEEKERS AFTER BEINGS OF INFINITE WISDOM TRAVEL CHECKLIST

Cut this out and keep it with you on your travels!

GOOD places to find wise old men	**BAD** places to find wise old men
•The Forbidden City of Ka-Tunga	•Hollywood
•The Gorge of the Golden Dragon	•Playing with themselves in 'adult' cinemas
•The Cavern of Nine Perils	•Tehran
•The Monastery of Utter Silence	•The Bowery
•The Temple of Solitude	•The Pentagon
•The Mountain of Jade	•Taking part in tobacco-spitting contests
•The Pinnacle of the Buddha	•Any courtroom

BEING ACCIDENTALLY HIT BY A POWER BEAM FROM ANOTHER WORLD

Don't rely on this method exclusively.

BECOMING ONE WITH THE UNIVERSE

A simple technique, in theory. You simply meditate until you understand the workings of the Universe, at which point you either obtain God-like powers or else start a cult that involves lots of scantily clad worshippers giving you tongue-baptisms and owning a fleet of tax-deductible Rolls-Royces. Either way you win!

The problem, in practice, is one of scale. Most people cannot comprehend the sheer size of the Universe and instead accidentally become one with the immediate vicinity.

For example, one would-be superhero, in his quest for the infinite, became one with New York City instead – and turned into a giant heap of shit that threatened to devour the rest of the state. Another became one with the United Nations – and is now incapable of doing anything when the need arises.

Even those attempting to 'get back to nature' in their quest have often proved to be incapable of surmounting this obstacle. Several people have become one with the Rockies and now have all the powers of a cretaceous rock stratum.

Less imaginative thinkers have met even more horrendous fates. Ronald Reagan became one with his own backside ... and ended up running the country for eight years. In a similar attempt, Warren Beatty became one with his groin...

BEING CAUGHT IN THE HEART OF A THERMONUCLEAR EXPLOSION.

Not recommended.

GETTING YOUR PARENTS SHOT DEAD IN FRONT OF YOUR EYES

At first, this might seem like a strange tactic, but if it was good enough to start *you know who* on one of the most successful crimefighting careers of all time, then it's certainly an avenue worth exploring!

Try persuading your parents to go on a nocturnal sightseeing walk with you around the South Bronx. Tell them it's for a school project...

DAD: I don't think we ought to be around here this time of night, son!

YOU: Oh, come on, dad! This is fabulous! Look over there – that's where George Washington used to live!

21

DAD: George Washington lived in a burned-out car?

GANGSTER: Alright, folks, this is a stick-up! Now just be cool. Give me yo' valuables and we's all gonna live to see another day...

MOM: He's got a gun, Henry!

YOU: Quick, dad, jump him!

DAD: WHAT?

GANGSTER: WHAT? Hey ... I got a gun, man! D-Don't try nothin'!

YOU: It's only a .32 calibre, dad! Go on, you can take him!

MOM: Be quiet, junior! Give him your wallet, Henry. He's obviously poor and homeless and needs the money...

GANGSTER: Right, right! Just gimme your wallet...

YOU: Give him nothing, dad! Kick him in the nuts! Rip his nipples off!

GANGSTER: Whut? Hey, just shut up, kid! Ya wallet, man! Quick!

YOU: You're dogmeat, pal! My dad's got a photographic memory! If you let him live, he'll pick you outta the line, no problem!

DAD: Look, here's my wallet. It's got $60 and some credit cards in it. Just take it and go.

YOU: Yeah, great plan, dad! Wait until he turns his back and then *wham*! Really let the little sucker have it!

GANGSTER: OK, lady, now yo' purse!

YOU: Dad! Dad! He's gonna ravish mom! Use yourself as a human shield!

GANGSTER: No I'm not! Just gimme yo' purse, lady!

MOM: Here's my purse. Now, just let us go.

GANGSTER: Thanks, folks! I'm outta here!

YOU: (SHOUTING) Hey, you dumb fuck son-of-a-bitch jerk-off dork-sucking dweeb!! My dad's got $32,000 in unmarked bills sewn into the lining of his jacket ... and you didn't get jackshit of it!

DAD: (SHOUTING) No, I haven't!

YOU: (SHOUTING) He's senile! 32,000 smackeroonies! And he's had your old lady! Five thousand times! At least! And she said he was a billion trillion times the man you are! Hey! Hey! Come back, short dick! Oh ... shit!

AND IF AT FIRST YOU DON'T SUCCEED...

DAD: Are you crazy, son? You could've got us all killed!

YOU: Er ... Gee, Dad, all the excitement's made me want to pee. Look, there's a public toilet over there. Let's go!

DAD: Me too, son, but I don't know. It looks awfully like a crack house to me...

YOU: (*Knocking on the door*) Hey, you guys in there! We wanna come inside and take a piss...

BEING ROCKETED TO EARTH AS AN INFANT

Are you a Star Baby? Do you feel in some way 'different' to those around you? Could you possibly be from *another planet*?
   It's not so far-fetched: How else can you explain Michael Jackson?
   You could, of course, ask your parents straight out: 'Am I from outer space?' But they might get too upset to answer, so the best thing to do is to quietly look for clues to your alien heritage and the vast powers that could be yours.

➡ Try gripping the icecubes in your freezer. Does a hologram of your true star-father appear?

➡ Were your mom and dad in their early eighties when they had you?

➡ Think back:
   – As a child, were you invulnerable to exploding artillery shells?
   – Did your parents give up on spanking you when you were naughty – and instead resort to backing the family car over you several times?
   – When you were naughty, did your mom and dad ever say, in a fit of exasperation, 'Jesus, I wish you'd go back to Alpha Centauri!'
   – Did you ever throw your rattle out of your buggy in a tantrum – and later learn that it had been found in Venezuela?
   – While other children were pulling the wings off flies, were you pulling the wings off commercial jetliners?

23

- Did you ever run away from home – and have to be retrieved by the Apollo program?
➡ Are your mom and dad Presbyterians – and yourself a crustacean?
➡ Do you get a feeling of homesickness when watching *Battlestar Galactica* reruns?
➡ Do you feel a special sense of kinship with Emo Phillips?
➡ Do you look different to your parents?
➡ Check out family records – you may be in for some surprises!

·MY FIRST YEAR·

My birth

My name is: Craig David Elkal-K4 Siegel

I was born on: April 14, 1973 (well he...
was found on that day, anyway)

Place: In a wheat field just off I-70, nr. Topeka, Kansas

When I was born I weighed: 172 lbs

I measured: 34 inches

My eyes were: Green and glowing

My family and friends

My parents: Starlord Cyber-X, Broodmate Shirah-K

My siblings: Sal-UI and Gar-II; Clone-Zygotes X423K & X427L

My friends: Ghengis, the Dobermann from next door and a
copperhead snake

My progress

I took my first steps at: 2 minutes

I ate my first food on: April 14, 1973

It was: A burning piece of coal from the open fire

My first drink from a cup was: Tractor oil

My first words were: Klaatu Barada Nikto

My first outing: Flew to Neptune while our backs were turned

My first books: 'Advanced Quantum Theory', 'Electrodynamics
and Relativity' (French edition)

My illnesses: Bruised leg after being run over by an 18-wheeler.
Slight cold after flying in the stratosphere without wearing a
hat. Mild diarrhea after sucking reservoir dry

I have been immunized against: Andromeda space plague;
Arcturian measles; Cygnian muto worms

My daytime pattern: Sleep, eat, run, fly, save someone's life,
eat, nap, dematerialize, lift something unbelievably heavy,
work out, break the sound barrier, sleep

My first mischief: Blowing the roofs off the neighbors' houses

25

NOPE, NONE OF THOSE METHODS WORKED FOR ME. (AND IF YOU THINK I'M WAITING AROUND TO GET STRUCK BY A POWER BEAM FROM ANOTHER WORLD, THINK AGAIN BUDDY!) DO I GET MY MONEY BACK?

Wait! Wait! Don't despair! There is still one foolproof method left: you can turn yourself into a CYBORG – half man, half killing machine!

Of course, no self-respecting, ethical and honest doctor will perform the necessary operation on you – which still leaves about 145,000 of them in the USA who'll do it if the money's right! But if you can't locate a crooked doctor or you're working to a tight budget, you'll have to perform the operation yourself.

THINGS TO DO PRIOR TO THE OPERATION:

1. Read a few books on surgical procedure
2. Get the wife and kids out of the house on some invented pretext, e.g.: 'Honey, your dad's just died. You and the kids had better fly up to Portland to be with your mother...'(Everyone's mother lives in Portland)
3. Tell the neighbors not to worry about any long and protracted screams coming from your house, accompanied by the sounds of industrial cutting equipment, because you've just rented Chainsaw Banshee Zombies on video for the evening
4. Assemble all the objects required as body parts (see blueprint)
5. Assemble all the surgical tools required to conduct the operation. These should include a petrol-driven chainsaw (or, at the very least, a hedgetrimmer), a breadknife, soldering iron, screwdriver, several clothes pegs (to staunch bleeding from major arteries during the operation), a blowtorch to cauterize various stubs and some large, non-porous receptical for you to be copiously sick into during the course of the operation
6. Scrub down the dining-room table and clear away any valuable or fragile items within thrashing distance
7. Put sheets down to protect the carpet
8. Pray

9. Anesthetize yourself as best you can, using one of the methods below:

➡ Drink 4 bottles of bourbon (although, when you finally sober up, you may find yourself half man–half curtains, half man–half kitchen unit, half man–half master bedroom, half man–half slippers ... or any one of a hundred other things!)

➡ Watch every episode of I Love Lucy in one sitting

➡ Watch one episode of any daytime soap

➡ Hit yourself repeatedly in the groin with a baseball bat until the pain of going through major body surgery seems to pale into insignificance by comparison

➡ Pretend to be Vanna White

➡ Headbutt the wall until you become confused

➡ Spend 15 minutes hyperventilating over the washing basket

➡ Swallow everything in the medicine chest (except, of course, the tube of hemorrhoid cream)

➡All of the above
10. Grit your teeth – and start cutting!

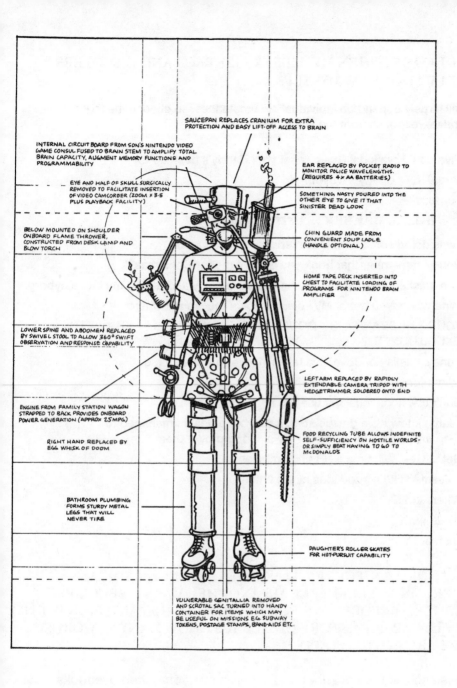

SAUCEPAN REPLACES CRANIUM FOR EXTRA
PROTECTION AND EASY LIFT-OFF ACCESS TO BRAIN

INTERNAL CIRCUIT BOARD FROM SON'S NINTENDO VIDEO
GAME CONSUL FUSED TO BRAIN STEM TO AMPLIFY TOTAL
BRAIN CAPACITY, AUGMENT MEMORY FUNCTIONS AND
PROGRAMMABILITY

EAR REPLACED BY POCKET RADIO TO
MONITOR POLICE WAVELENGTHS.
(REQUIRES 4 x AA BATTERIES)

EYE AND HALF OF SKULL SURGICALLY
REMOVED TO FACILITATE INSERTION
OF VIDEO CAMCORDER (ZOOM x 3·5
PLUS PLAYBACK FACILITY)

SOMETHING NASTY POURED INTO THE
OTHER EYE TO GIVE IT THAT
SINISTER DEAD LOOK

BELOW MOUNTED ON SHOULDER
ONBOARD FLAME THROWER,
CONSTRUCTED FROM DESK LAMP AND
BLOW TORCH

CHIN GUARD MADE FROM
CONVENIENT SOUP LADLE
(HANDLE OPTIONAL)

HOME TAPE DECK INSERTED INTO
CHEST TO FACILITATE LOADING OF
PROGRAMS FOR NINTENDO BRAIN
AMPLIFIER

LOWER SPINE AND ABDOMEN REPLACED
BY SWIVEL STOOL TO ALLOW 360° SWIFT
OBSERVATION AND RESPONSE CAPABILITY

LEFT ARM REPLACED BY RAPIDLY
EXTENDABLE CAMERA TRIPOD WITH
HEDGETRIMMER SOLDERED ONTO END

ENGINE FROM FAMILY STATION WAGON
STRAPPED TO BACK PROVIDES ONBOARD
POWER GENERATION (APPROX 25 MPG.)

RIGHT HAND REPLACED BY
EGG WHISK OF DOOM

FOOD RECYCLING TUBE ALLOWS INDEFINITE
SELF-SUFFICIENCY ON HOSTILE WORLDS-
OR SIMPLY BEAT HAVING TO GO TO
McDONALD'S

BATHROOM PLUMBING
FORMS STURDY METAL
LEGS THAT WILL
NEVER TIRE

DAUGHTER'S ROLLER SKATES
FOR HOT-PURSUIT CAPABILITY

VULNERABLE GENITALLIA REMOVED
AND SCROTAL SAC TURNED INTO HANDY
CONTAINER FOR ITEMS WHICH MAY
BE USEFUL ON MISSIONS E.G. SUBWAY
TOKENS, POSTAGE STAMPS, BAND-AIDS ETC.

WHAT DO I SAY WHEN MY WIFE COMES BACK AND DISCOVERS WHAT I'VE DONE TO MYSELF?

This will largely depend on individual circumstances, so choose the most appropriate response from the suggestions below.

➡ 'Hiya hon! Hiya kids! Guess what your daddy's been up to!'

➡ '*Ta-da*! Your daddy's a cyborg!'

➡ 'Surprise!'

➡ **'Gaaaa ... akkkkk ... urrrrgggghh!'**

➡ 'I was doing some household repairs – and slipped!'

➡ 'Honey, remember that book you bought me for Christmas?'

➡ 'Two masked men broke in while you were away and turned me into a cyborg.'

➡ 'Mind where you tread. My spleen's down there somewhere.'

➡ 'YOUR – HUSBAND – IS – GONE – MRS FLYNN – I – AM – KB 12 – THE – EXECUTIONER!!!'

➡ 'Honey, this is goodbye. I've fallen in love with the stereo.'

➡ 'I did it for you!'

➡ 'Don't cry, hon; You'll get used to it!'

➡ 'Yeah, I know it's a drastic step, babe, but at least I managed to keep my pecker. Look, it's on the sideboard over there.'

➡ 'Get ... Get ... Get me a f@#$ing ambulance!'

➡ 'It seemed like a good idea at the time...'

➡ 'Where am I?'

➡ '*What* am I?!'

➡ 'Trick or treat!'

WHOA! HOLD ON THERE! I'M NOT PERFORMING RADICAL SURGERY ON MYSELF! TELL ME ANOTHER WAY TO BECOME A SUPERHERO BEFORE I ASK FOR MY MONEY BACK (AND POINT OUT TO MY LOCAL BOOKSTORE OWNER JUST HOW MANY 'F' WORDS THERE ARE IN THIS BOOK)...

There is another type of superhero – a type everyone often overlooks – the Jungle Lord.

A Jungle Lords' powers are limited to being able to talk to animals which is, let's face it, pretty useless. What are you ever going to have to say to a Thompson's Gazelle? What could hippopotami know that could be worth listening to? But, if you've run out of other options, at least it's fairly easy to become a Jungle Lord.

All you have to do is live through a plane crash in some remote region of the globe and then be brought up by wild animals (that's 'brought up' as in 'raised', not as in 'eaten and then regurgitated').

Be very choosy, though, about the animals you let adopt you. Mowgli was fine among the wolves and Tarzan with the apes, but there have been a host of less successful Jungle Lords who have long since vanished into utter obscurity...

TOMARR OF THE MOLLUSCS
By Harry K. Dietrich

As he grew, Tomarr experienced all the riches that filled the life of a Mollusc. Swiftly, he began to imitate a limpet's stoic fortitude in the face of terrible danger from predatory sea birds and his courage grew. From the Molluscs, he gained a unique code of bravery and, like them, did not run when death swooped down on thrashing wings to rend and tear and crack, but stayed defiantly still.

The greater virtue of patience he learned from Uk, the oldest and wisest limpet of them all. Uk had adopted Tomarr as his own, and Tomarr knew that he would one day assume the privileged position in the shallow rock pool that Uk now occupied. They were inseparable. Many were the days they would sit together under the relentless African sun, silent and unmoving.

Yes, from Uk above all he learned patience and found an inner peace. And then all was silence and stillness and very, very little happened over the next twenty-seven years, mainly because Tomarr had starved to death twenty six years earlier.

FROM TARZAN RIP-OFF QUARTERLY (1920)

LYRIC OF THE MAN-EATING MANGAL TIGERS

By T. V. Donald

REALISTIC TALES (1921)

MIRKI OF THE DOLPHINS

By Nancy Fellows

AMAZINGLY SHORT STORIES (1922)

SVEN OF THE LEMMINGS

By Olaf Jacobson

ALL-LEMMING ADVENTURE (1928)

OK, IM SUPERPOWERED! CAN I TRASH THE BAD GUYS NOW?

You missed out the apostrophe on I'm...

WHO GIVES A SH#$? CAN I TRASH THE BAD GUYS NOW?

No. First you must understand your superpowers and exactly what you can hope to achieve with them.
Here's a brief and useful guide to the kinds of things your superpowers will allow you to accomplish.

THIS HAD BETTER NOT BE A LONG SECTION! I WANNA GET ON TO KICKING SOME SUPERVILLAIN BUTT!

Have patience! Right, first of all, we have...

SUPERSTRENGTH

One of the most common powers – and a category that includes everything from being able to hurl whole express trains into orbit right through to being able to remove screw top lids from bottles without having to give up and make lame excuses about your hands being all sweaty and slippery.
The drawback with superstrength is that your intelligence *must* decrease in direct proportion to your prowess, so that the more muscles you have, the more stupid you become ... or what is commonly referred to, in the medical world, as the Dolph Lundgren Syndrome.
In this equation, power levels equate to the following grades of retained intelligence:

Power Level One:	**Average intelligence**
Power Level Two:	**Government-employee level of intelligence**
Power Level Three:	**Higher primate (e.g. Orang-Utan)**
Power Level Four:	**Sports star (track or field)**
Power Level Five:	**Amoeboid intelligence only**
Power Level Six:	**Brain death, Dan Quayle**

INVISIBILITY

Invisibility is one of the safest powers of all to possess, not only because you can't be seen to shoot at but also because you can wrap up in lots of woollies on a cold day without looking like a cissy and avoid getting a potentially nasty chill.

Invisibility also means you can use subterfuge and cunning to subdue your foes rather than slugging it out with them. For example, you can cause gangs of villains to fight among themselves by sneaking into their hideout and wreaking havoc, like so...

LEFTY: Right, let's divide up the loot!

SCARFACE: Sure ... Hey! You just pinched my ass!

LEFTY: In your dreams!

SCARFACE: Hey! Leave my goddam ass alone, willya?

LEFTY: I wouldn't touch your ass if it wuz solid gold!

SCARFACE: Well, I don't see nobody else around here within reach of m ass!

LEFTY: OK, look, fifty for you ... an' fifty for me. Fifty for you...

SCARFACE: You just whispered, 'Drop your pants, I love you, you big garbonza!' right in my ear!

LEFTY: What are you talk– Hey! What's that wad of fifty-dollar bills suddenly doin' in your pocket? You're trying to rip me off!

SCARFACE: Jeez! Now you're strokin'my balls!

LEFTY: Turn out ya pockets, asswipe!

SCARFACE: Do it yaself! You got ya goddam hand down one!

BANG! BANG!

... Another mission successfully accomplished!

TELEPATHY

Telepathy is a useful ability to have in combat. For example, reading yo opponent's mind when he's thinking, 'I'm going to punch him now!' giv you a chance to parry his blow! Equally, being able to read, 'I'm going hit him with this girder!' in your opponent's mind gives you time to dod and 'I'm going to rip Captain Psyche's nuts off, grind them into paste a then serve them up to him on a savory cracker!' gives you the chance run for your life!

Having telepathic powers also means that no one will ever be able t successfully lie to you again – not even a lawyer. The downside of it all that you may start picking up thoughts you didn't want to hear, like...

➡ Oh, it's only Captain Psyche! For a minute there I thought I'd have to fight a *proper* superhero!

➡ That superhero's got a *really* small bulge in his tights

➡ I wonder if he realizes what a dildo he looks in that costume

➡ What are those funny marks on the back of his tights?

➡ Next time we have a superteam meeting, let's not invite that twat Captain Psyche

➡ Jeez! He's such a *feeb* in bed...

SUPERSPEED

Things that superspeed is useful for:

➡ Running so fast that you travel into the future

➡ Running fast in a circle, so that your enemies are swept up in a cyclone

➡ Vibrating your body's molecules so fast you can move through solid objects

➡ Landing eight and a half million punches on an opponent's jaw in four milliseconds

➡ Racing Captain Superswift around the globe in a particularly dull issue of your own comic

➡ Racing over to Egypt, seeing the pyramids – and then getting the hell out before you contract something

➡ Dashing out to defeat a supervillain – and getting back before your girlfriend realizes you were gone ... even though you were making love at the time...

➡ Changing into your costume on a bitterly cold day

➡ Having a neat costume with a lightning bolt, tornado, meteor, cheetah or some other impressive symbol on the chest

➡ Writing a manuscript to most publishers' deadlines

Things that superspeed is *not* useful for:

➡ Working for the government

➡ Avoiding dog shit on the sidewalk dead ahead

X-RAY VISION

Every young boy's dream ... or is it? Remember those small ads in the comics offering an X-Ray Vision-o-Scope and the fantasies you had about being able to see into the girls' locker room after gym? Oh yes, you do.

Unfortunately, X-ray vision doesn't work like that. You see *through* people.

So, after you gain this power, you're not going to wander around looking at girls thinking, 'Yow! What a pair of kidneys!', 'Look at the *cerebellum* on that!' or 'I'd love to get my hands around her fibias'. Right?

So you're going to use the power properly, to fight crime instead? Wrong.

How do you stop supervillains, armed only with an intimate knowledge of their internal physiognomy? In a really desperate situation, you could try worrying them by saying something like, 'Hey Commander Kruel, you really should get that spleen seen to. It could be inflamed!' or 'What's that dark shadow over your left lung, Kong The Merciless? I'd consult a specialist...'

But if this is your sole superpower, best to stick to your day job.

POWER OVER THE ANT

Most people who develop this superpower usually throw up their hands in despair and cry, 'What am I supposed to do with control over ants? Ruin supervillains' picnics?'

Well, that's not a bad start! Many supervillains do enjoy picnics on their days off and can be mightily upset if their day is spoiled!

However, that's just the beginning of the potential of having an ant army at your disposal! Ants have far more of a role to play in the fight against evil than you might credit them for and, with you to lead them, there is virtually no limit to what they can achieve!

A) They can hide supervillains' contact lenses!

B) They can be instructed to climb inside a supervillain's socks and tickle his feet, thereby distracting him enough for you to deliver the knock-out punch!

C) You can use your ants to move a supervillain's getaway car while he's robbing the bank! (But this will require an awful lot of them...)

D) Being acrobatic by nature, ants can bounce up and down on a supervillain's eyelids – tricking him into thinking he feels tired!

E) They can absolutely devastate a supervillain's gravel path by removing the bits of gravel from it!

F) They can get into supervillains' cupboards – and eat all the sugar!

G) They can swop over lo-cal sugar for ordinary sugar – thereby ruining any supervillain's attempts to diet and making him slow and lethargic in combat – as well as ashamed to appear in costume!

H) They can surreptitiously pack earwax into a supervillain's ears, so he can't hear you sneaking up behind him!

I) They can help you to disguise yourself on undercover missions – by forming themselves into sideburns or a large black wart on the end of your nose!

J) They can build ant hills in the supervillain's front garden – thereby reducing his property value!

K) Flying Ants can drop grains of sugar into the supervillain's hair – and make him think that he's got dandruff! (This is especially effective if he wears a dark costume or cape)

L) They can crawl up his trouser leg and squirt formic acid all over his private parts!

M) PLUS, any supervillain made of jam or any other form of fruit preserve is especially vulnerable to your miniscule pals! So be sure that your personal 'Rogues' Gallery' includes plenty of villains like The Incredible Marmalade Man, The Raspberry Skull and The Fruity Reaper!

COSMIC POWERS

The mightiest powers of all! You are a conduit, with all the elemental forces of the universe channeled through your body! You have the powers to devastate entire worlds, divert the course of comets, boil suns until they go supernova ... and if you think any supervillain is going to fight you with powers like that – forget it!

Once word gets around, even supervillains in teams won't try to defeat you. To maintain your heroic stature, you'll have to deliberately pick fights.

A word of warning: Be *very careful* not to get careless in your desperation for a scrap. It could have dire consequences!

CAPTAIN COSMIC: Alright, Crime Kings, surrender now!

POLECAT: Yep, alright.

CAPTAIN COSMIC: What?

POLECAT: You said, 'Surrender.' Seems perfectly reasonable to me, right, boys?

HELLFIST: Hey, fine by me!

THE INVINCIBLE DYNAMO: Sure!

KAPTAIN NAZI: Jawohl, Herr Kapitän!

CAPTAIN COSMIC: What? I Mean ... Don't you want a fight first?

HELLFIST: No, no. You just take us in. I'd love to do some time!

THE INVINCIBLE DYNAMO: Yeah, who wants ta be masters of the world anyway? That's for saps!

CAPTAIN COSMIC: Oh, go on.

HELLFIST: No!

CAPTAIN COSMIC: Look, look, I won't use my Mega Rod. I promise.

POLECAT: No, I'm sorry. Just take us in ... and throw away the key!

CAPTAIN COSMIC: Wait! One hand tied behind my back ... two! No *cosmic power kicks...*

HELLFIST: No, we're quite happy to come quietly, thank you all the same.

CAPTAIN COSMIC: How, what about if I just use one finger? A toe? My eyebrows?

POLECAT: We're not stupid enough to tackle both of your eyebrows, Captain Cosmic!

CAPTAIN COSMIC: I'll shave one! Oh, go on, go on, go on! Say yes!

POLECAT: No earlobes?

CAPTAIN COSMIC: No earlobes, I promise.

POLECAT: Backs of knees?

CAPTAIN COSMIC: Cross my heart and hope to die!

POLECAT: Nape? Skin flakings? Earwax? Sweat? Mons pubis? Verruca?

CAPTAIN COSMIC: Scout's honour! Just one eyebrow.

POLECAT: What do you think, Crime Kings?

CRIME KINGS: Yeah, let's get him!!!!!!!!!

CAPTAIN COSMIC: Fools! One eyebrow contains the energy of a million exploding galaxies! You didn't stand a chance! (*Pause.*) Well, that wasn't much of a fight.I don't know why I bothered, really ... Hello, where did Earth go to all of a sudden? *Oh, sh#:..*

SUPER DIARRHEA

There is no such superpower. You've probably just eaten at a Mexican restaurant recently.

SUPER HEARING

Not the most useful superpower to possess. You can hear when a crime is being committed anywhere in the city ... but when you get there, it doesn't really help you do anything about it!

You can't deflect bullets with your ear lobes; you can't listen a supervillain into submission, and all he has to do is raise his voice to pop your eardrums.

Plus have you ever thought about what a city sounds like to someone with superhearing ... all the farting, belching, sneezing, sniffing, and deadly dull conversations that fill a vast metropolis? Having to listen to every TV channel simultaneously, all those Boom Boxes – and one and a half million fervent Republicans all spouting off? The endless arguments, small talk, abuse, crying ... and five million people all making disgusting smacking noises every lunchtime?

Superhearing is a nightmare. What's more, your ears are so sensitive it's usually impossible to differentiate between someone talking to you and conversations going on five miles away, so a typical conversation might go like this:

OLD LADY: Oh, Captain Audio! Thank goodness! Some nasty men just stole my purse!

CAPTAIN AUDIO: Who are you calling a motherfucker?

OLD LADY: What?

CAPTAIN AUDIO: Oh, um ... just take next left and it's down two blocks.

OLD LADY: Are you alright, young man?

CAPTAIN AUDIO: What are you talking about? That's not my car!

OLD LADY: Should I call an ambulance for you?

CAPTAIN AUDIO: Marvin? *Who's Marvin?*

OLD LADY: Oh dear! Are you severely injured in the head?

CAPTAIN AUDIO: Er ... no ... ma'am. I'm fine! How can I help you?

OLD LADY: Oh, thank goodness! Captain Audio, some bad men just stole my purse!

CAPTAIN AUDIO: Yeah, and you can swivel on it too, buddy!

OLD LADY: Oh, fe#$ this. I'm calling a cop.

STRETCHING POWERS

Admit it. For as long as you can remember, you've longed for the woman in your life to say, 'Oh! That's so colossally, unimaginably huge that nothing short of the Brooklyn Tunnel is capable of taking it! Safe sex would require at least eight to ten deflated Navy Blimps all sewn together! You could lay that thing across the East River and charge commuters a toll to drive over it!'

Haven't you? Well, welcome to the superpower that everyone dreams of getting! With such a power, you may find yourself left with very little free time in which to fight crime and avenge the wronged – but who cares, right?

If you do embark on a crimefighting career, be under no illusion! Other superheroes are going to hate your guts!! You'll never be invited to join superteams or participate in Crossovers and Secret Wars, and you'll be the first one they suspect of being a traitorous Rigelian Shape Shifting Man-Droid on the flimsiest of pretexts and consequently beat up en masse whenever the opportunity arises.

One final warning: prolonged use of stretching powers may lead to your costume going all baggy at the knees. Use with care!

AQUATIC POWERS

Of little use if you are sworn to protect somewhere like Omaha from evildoers – and of little use in general. Very few crimes actually take place beneath the waves, since there are no banks to rob or research laboratories to raid. You could, of course, swear that no harm shall befall the herring in your care or try to thwart the evil schemes of diabolical lobsters bent on world domination – but after a while you'll start to feel silly (and cold) and quit.

FLIGHT

It's great to fly under your own powers, secure in the knowledge that your life isn't in the hands of some guy who's just stuffed last month's pay cheque up his nose and currently thinks that his co-pilot is turning into some kind of giant blond spider.

You can smoke if you want to. You won't be grounded because the chief steward's boyfriend has just left him and he won't come out of the toilet, or be abruptly rerouted via Wichita, St Paul and Anchorage for no good reason whatsoever (while your luggage is rerouted via Osaka, Kuala Lumpur and Seville – and then scattered between Kabul, Santiago and Mombasa).

SHAPECHANGING POWERS

With the ability to assume the identity of anybody else, you'll make the perfect undercover agent, touring the underworld dives in search of your prey!

However, before you start here are some operational rules.

1. NEVER IMPERSONATE AN OBJECT WHEN YOU WANT INFORMATION

YOU: Hey, any of you guys seen Dutch Mclean hanging around here?

THUG #1: Hey, you guys! This Coke machine just spoke ta me!

THUG #2: Whutchu been smokin', man? Talkin' Coke machine? Crap!

YOU: So, you got something for me or ... Hey! Watch where you're shoving that quarter, pal! Ouch! Ooooooooooooooooh!

THUG #1: Goddam machine ate my money and didn't give me no can, man! Take that! Come on, you son of a bitch!! Gimme my Coke!

YOU: Ooof! Arrrgh! Youch! Urrrgh!

2. DON'T CHOOSE TO IMPERSONATE SOMEONE UNLIKELY

YOU: Hey, bartender! I'm looking for Lefty Guccione. Could be worth a ten spot...

BARTENDER: Lefty, huh? Who wants ta know?

YOU: William Shatner. Now, you got something for me or what?

3. DON'T IMPERSONATE SOMEONE DEAD

YOU: Yo! You Mugsy Malone?

MALONE: What if I am?

YOU: We gotta talk.

MALONE: Hey, I recognize ya! You're Indira Gandhi!

YOU: Yup! That's my name. Don't wear it out. Let's talk somewhere quieter.

MALONE: But you're dead, lady!

YOU: So I got better already! I don't do Head of Stating no more. Now I've set up in business for myself an' I need some info!

MALONE: Hey! You ain't no ex-Prime Minister of India! You're ... Captain Proteus! Get him, boys!

YOU: Oh poo!

4. NEVER IMPERSONATE YOUR MOM WHEN YOU WANT INFORMATION

YOU: Hi, boys! I was just doing my shopping and I thought I'd pop by and see if Razors DiSteffano was in today!

THUG: Huh? What's an old lady like you want wid Razors?

YOU: Ah ... he's got this great recipe for Apple Bake he's promised to let me have ... and I wanted to see if he was free to help me with my garage sale next Saturday.

THUG: Uh, lady, ya sure ya got da right Razors here?

YOU: Oh yes. About 6'4"... scar here to here. Works for the Raffia brothers ... such nice boys. Always so well dressed. I've known Razors ever since he joined our Valley Sewing Circle...

THUG: Wait a goddam minute! You ain't no old lady! Hey, it's Captain Proteus! Sic him boys!

5. NEVER IMPERSONATE YOURSELF

It doesn't make sense.

SUPERBREATH

Superbreath is an oft derided power, yet, combined with a simple medical condition such as halitosis or a predilection for traditional Turkish cuisine, it can be deployed to quite staggering effect in the fight against crime.

One warning: don't be tempted to call yourself anything like Captain Blow Job. You'll only attract the *wrong* sort of 'Rogues' Gallery'.

Oh yes, whatever you do, don't ever, ever blow in your girlfriend's ear...

TRANSFORMATION POWERS

Useful things to be able to transform yourself into:

➡ Steel
➡ Any of the elements
➡ Ferocious jungle beasts
➡ Gases
➡ A giant
➡ A typhoon

Useless things to be able to transform yourself into:

➡ French toast
➡ Your younger brother
➡ Septicemia
➡ Anyone on the FBI's 'Most Wanted' list
➡ Individual letters of the alphabet
➡ Drool
➡ Dog Poo
➡ Skimmed milk
➡ 20th century poets...

THAT'S IT, ISN'T IT? FOR SURE THIS TIME! WATCH OUT SUPERVILLAINS! YOUR LAW-BREAKING ASS IS MINE!

Sorry, that's just the end of chapter 1. Here comes chapter 2 now...

SECRET IDENTITIES

RIGHT, WHAT SHALL I CALL MYSELF?

Choosing your name is probably the most important decision you'll ever have to make as a costumed crimefighter... and it's worth taking some time to think it through.

Work it out logically. Don't decide on the first thing that comes to mind. There are already far too many lazy superheroes who made this mistake and who are now running about with names like Mr Tiffany Naked and Captain I-Wonder-What's-For-Dinner. Captain Christ-Who-Just-Farted-In-Here is another, particularly sad, example.

Let's establish some ground rules...

1. Don't call yourself by your real name,.e.g. Mr Fred Pinchuck, Mr Harry Rabinowitz, The Amazing Stevie Foster.
2. Equally, don't call yourself by someone else's real name, e.g. Mr Teddy Kennedy, The Amazing Oliver North, Captain Dean Martin.
3. Choose a name that suggests power, heroism and prowess, e.g. Captain Power, Thunderman, Mr Invincible, Justiceman.
4. But don't labour the point, e.g. Mr So-Fo#%ing-Powerful-Don't-Even-Think-About-It-Buddy.
5. Then again, don't be too modest, e.g. Mr Pretty Good, Captain So-So, The Fairly Incredible Mr Universe.
6. Equally, don't choose a name which is actually detrimental to your crimefighting image, e.g. Captain Spongecake, Mr Asshole, The Yellow Streak, The Purple Helmet, Mr Evil, Captain Goebbels, Mr Shit-For-Brains.
7. Don't choose a name with a sexual double meaning. For example, The AC/DC Man is not a good name for a superhero with electrical powers.
   Likewise, if you combine superspeed with prodigious leaping powers, call yourself something like Speed-Frog instead of The Quick Jump ... and so on.
8. Don't choose the name of an existing superhero unless you have lots of money and enjoy fighting litigation instead of supervillains. (This goes double if you have a 'rude' or otherwise 'disreputable' power which some people may find offensive, such as buttocks that double as throwing stars.)
9. It's no use calling yourself something like Captain Invincible if your only power is control over Hostess Twinkies and you suffer from a congenital hole-in-the-heart condition. It's just asking for trouble.
10. Don't call yourself The Invisible Boy ... if you're not.
11. Don't call yourself The Invisible Boy ... if you're a girl.
12. Don't call yourself Invisible Lady ... if you're a man – even if you do feel like you're a woman trapped in a man's body.
13. Don't give away any important information in your name, e.g The Glass Jaw, Captain Vulnerable To Strontium 90.
14. Don't call yourself The Green Avenger if you wear an orange costume. You'll confuse people.

I'VE THOUGHT UP A NAME FOR MYSELF. NOW I NEED A COSTUME. WHERE CAN I BUY ONE FROM?

You can't. You'll have to design and sew your own costume.

I CAN'T SEW.

Learn.

I AIN'T NEVER DONE NO DRESS DESIGNING BEFORE. WHAT SHOULD MY COSTUME BE LIKE?

➡ Something dark, to strike fear into the hearts of men

➡ Something colorful - to enhance your merchandising potential

➡ Something you can change in and out of - fast!

➡ Something bulletproof

➡ Something woven from Kevlar to deflect Ninja death stars

➡ Something warm in the winter

➡ Something made from muscle (and genital) enhancing skintight Spandex

AND WHAT SHOULD I AVOID WHEN I'M DESIGNING MY COSTUME?

➡ Too much embroidery - a finished costume (however breathtaking) could take years!

➡ A face mask that doesn't hide your face

➡ A face mask you can't see out of

➡ A face mask - and nothing else

➡ Anything you have to knit yourself

➡ Anything that's highly inflammable

➡ Anything patched together from lace doilies

➡ Anything incorporating a Bullseye motif over the heart

➡ Anything made out of horsehair

➡ Anything skimpy

➡ Anything see-through

➡ Anything shocking pink with sequins

➡ Anything that scuffs easily or needs dry cleaning

➡ Anything that looks like you bought it at K-Mart or Woolworths.

➡ Anything white (if you operate at night)

➡ Anything white (if you're called something like 'The Black Avenger')

➡ Anything white if you have aqua powers - (because your costume will become transparent and you won't be able to climb out of the water)

- Hoops - they'll make you look fat
- Corduroy
- Nylon (you'll get nasty static shocks every time you try to fight Metal Men)
- A costume that's so tight you rip it every time you throw a punch
- A costume that's so tight they can tell your religion
- A costume design that requires you to wear your underpants over your tights (people have been laughing at superheroes for this for over forty years, but the message doesn't seem to sink in)
- Anything that involves a leotard of some description
- Incontinence knickers
- A costume that's really an alien space parasite pretending to be a costume
- Anything even slightly resembling a saucy French Maid's outfit
- Anything two sizes too big
- Flares
- Sewing your costume during breaks at the construction site or pit head

NOW I'VE GOT A NAME...AND A COSTUME. WHAT'S NEXT?

When you're not a superhero, you'll need to blend back into civilian life...and that civilian identity may well be the key to your success or failure as a superhero. Choose your civilian identity wisely.

HOLD ON! I'M ALREADY SOMEBODY! THAT'S WHO I'M GOING TO BE WHEN I'M NOT SAVING THE UNIVERSE AND STUFF!

But are you the right kind of somebody? Certain types of people are far more suited to being the alter-ego of superheroes than others. If you're not one of the types below, you ought to seriously consider changing who you are...

MILLIONAIRE PLAYBOY

No-one's denying that it's going to be tough, living the life of an idle millionaire playboy, but you'll just have to try...

Force yourself to soak your feet in Dom Perignon, sleep with 150 different beautiful women every week, blow your nose on Picasso sketches if there's no Kleenex to hand (hell, who'll notice?) and wreck your Ferrari Testarossa while coked out of your skull and get off 'cos the judge is a golfing buddy. But, weighed against this hell on Earth, do remember that being a millionaire playboy gives you a number of unique crimefighting advantages over the other poor working slobs in the business...

➡ If a terrifying Sea Behemoth appears from beneath the waves and he threatens the Bahamas, chances are you'll be right on the spot to stop it!

➡ If Jackie Onassis ever suddenly turns into a three hundred foot Rampaging Swamp Beast and starts to menace Midtown Manhattan, you'll be alerted instantly - because you live in the apartment next door!

➡ The next time Jewel King and his gang decide to raid Tiffany's - you could very well be inside (buying a diamond encrusted dick-wiper or something) - and will catch him totally by surprise!

➡ If an alien shapeshifter impersonates Bruce Willis as part of an insidious masterplan to take over the world, you'll see through the deception immediately...because you know Bruce so well!

➡ You can use your fabulous wealth on the battlefield as well as in your secret identity, like so...

DR DEMONIAC: Ha, you're surrounded, Captain! Get him, my loyal cronies!

CAPTAIN Z: Hey, hold on, cronies! How much is this geek paying you guys?

CRONEY #1: Er...$200 a week...

CRONEY #2: Plus we get to keep any tips...only we don't get no tips...

DR DEMONIAC: What are you waiting for, fools? Kill him! Kill him!

CRONEY #3: An' we haveta go dutch on gas for the Demoniacmobile an' buy our own costumes an' ray guns - an' they ain't cheap!

DR DEMONIAC: Kill him! Kill him, you cretins!

CAPTAIN Z: How'd you boys like to work for me instead? 600 bucks a week!

CRONEY #1: I...I dunno...

CAPTAIN Z: Free Medical insurance, 15 days paid leave. I'll respect all Jewish holidays...

CRONEY #3: That's good...the Doc wouldn't even give us Chanukah. My ma'll never let me hear the end of that...

CRONEY #1: Whut about pension plans?

CAPTAIN Z: Non-contributory, of course. Employee Assistance Scheme...

DR DEMONIAC: Kill him! Kill him! Kill him! Kill him!

CAPTAIN Z: Regular performance-based salary reviews. Opportunities for overtime at time and a half...Well, are you boys in ?

CRONIES: YEAH!

DR DEMONIAC: Jesus H Christ! I must have the worst cronies in the business!

CAPTAIN Z: That's because I already hired all the rest! Give up, Doc! You won't be able to afford a gang of cronies in future!

DR DEMONIAC: Curse You, Captain Z! I'll import cheap labor cronies! I'll defeat you yet, you rich bastard!

CAPTAIN Z: Get him, *my* cronies!

DR DEMONIAC: YAAAARGH!...$225!...ARRRRGH!....And preferential loans for your costumes and hardware! EUURRRGH! No! Stop! Stop! Paid Chanukah leave...NOOOOOOOOOOOOOO!

MILD-MANNERED REPORTER

As a mild-mannered reporter, you'll have an excuse for snooping around and getting into the kind of scrapes from which super-adventures just seem to materialise!

Becoming a reporter is easy (you just work as one for a newspaper), but being mild-mannered, if it's not in your blood, is another matter.
Try to remember the following rules:

THINGS MILD-MANNERED MEN DO
➡ Wash their hands after going to the toilet
➡ Use public transport (but not after dark)
➡ Hold doors open for ladies (but blush and stammer if they say thanks)
➡ Wait in line
➡ Wear sensible shoes
➡ Look both ways before crossing a busy street
➡ Snuggle up with a good book
➡ Stay late at the office whenever it's necessary (and even when it's not)
➡ Pay for everything on a date (if they get dates, that is)
➡ Carry a raincoat and an umbrella – just in case.
➡ Look forward to the next issue of Reader's Digest
➡ Visit their parents every Easter and Christmas vacation
➡ Take sandwiches to the office everyday
➡ Send their aunties Christmas cards
➡ Wear unflattering glasses
➡ Come from small towns
➡ Eat quiche

THINGS MILD-MANNERED MEN *DON'T* DO
➡ Ride a nitro-burning Harley Drag bike
➡ See how far they can spit
➡ Play Quarterback for The Washington Redskins
➡ Blow their wages on *Blow*
➡ Have a Mohican haircut
➡ Read 'Big Boobie Action' or 'Hot Shaven Leather Bitches Special'
➡ Head-butt police cars on a dare
➡ Waggle their tongues at waitresses across a crowded restaurant
➡ Touch below the waist on a first date
➡ Take pleasure in farting in public
➡ Know all the words to Sweet Child Of Mine
➡ Call women 'chicks', 'broads' or 'pussy'.
➡ Hang out on 42nd Street, whispering, 'Yo Blood, check *this* out!'
➡ Pinch nuns' bottoms
➡ Ask eleven greasers what the fuck they think they're looking at.
➡ Belch to the tune of The Marine's Hymn

A POLITICIAN

Everyone knows that a politician is far more likely to be a supervillain if anything - so this secret identity is almost unguessable!

Plus, you can disappear any time you like and people will just assume you've gone off to pay your regular visit to Madame Syn's Washington Dungeon and Spanking Parlour, dry out at some clinic or are snuggling up to two high school girls and a pound of prime Peruvian Flake in some hotel room in The Bahamas, courtesy of your local major munitions manufacturer or oil baron.

ELECTRONICS GENIUS

If you're a teenager, then this is the ideal secret identity for you! Everyone knows that electronics geniuses are into doing some pretty eccentric things in their rooms, like tinkering with *gizmos*, building *doohickeys* and masturbating themselves stupid whenever their moms go out to the stores.

So, as an electronics genius, you can build all the kind of equipment you need to defeat even the most technologically advanced of supervillains, without anybody asking what you're doing - because they really don't want to know, having automatically assumed that its going to be ultra-ultra mega tedious and mind-bleedingly boring, whatever it is.

LAWYER

As a lawyer, you get to mingle with cops and crooks close up and see how the law really works. You make useful underworld contacts, build relationships with the police department and pocket truly astronomical sums of cash with which you can fight crime!

Plus nobody would ever believe that a lawyer would do anything for a motive other than financial gain!

It's the perfect training...and the perfect cover! There's an old joke about lawyers needing to practice: Here's how you can practice being a convincing lawyer ...

➡ Help your parents sort out a legal problem and charge them (preferably double)
➡ Sell your mother to the arabs
➡ Sell your father to the arabs
➡ Sell your family pet to the arabs
➡ Take coins from your poor blind granny's purse...and replace them with broken glass
➡ Raid the State Penitentiary - and let out as many dangerous criminals as you can. If the cops catch you, simply say you're a lawyer and you're just doing your job
➡ Bring yourself to orgasm by sniffing $100 bills
➡ Taunt blind, orphaned unipeds - whenever the opportunity arises
➡ Be disproportionately cruel to small animals
➡ Find a child alone in its pram. Take his teddy and zippo it in front of his eyes
➡ When someone asks you any legal question, like even if the answer is unbelievably cut and dried, say 'well, it depends...'
➡ Deliberately drag out painful divorce proceedings - just so you can buy a new BMW

'I'm a lawyer in my secret identity, but I'm starting to get confused. As Captain Milwaukee, I apprehend villains by battling them into submission - but then as 'Myself', I get them set free again on the grounds of wrongful arrest and use of excessive force.

'My Arch Enemy Dr Mutant Insectivold is earning me a small fortune; I've got him off a total of 72 times now!'

Thundercrack,
Chevy Chase, MD

'Yes, I'd recommend being a lawyer in your secret identity. That'll be $880 plus state tax. You can pay the receptionist on the way out.'

Captain Triumphant,
Long Island, NY

EXTRA CUNNING CIVILIAN IDENTITIES

A MAN ON A LIFE SUPPORT MACHINE

➡ They won't believe you're physically capable

A DRUNKEN BUM

➡ They won't believe you're mentally capable

DAN QUAYLE

➡ They won't believe you're physically or mentally capable

IOWA

➡ no-one cares about Iowa, so you'll be able to go about your activities unnoticed!

THEY SOUND GREAT, ESPECIALLY THE LAST ONE. BUT HOW DO I PRETEND TO BE IOWA?

Disguise yourself as 56,290 square miles of flat, unexceptional farmland, dotted with towns no-one's ever heard of, make sure that there's ten pigs and 750 potatoes per head of population and then do nothing remarkable so that no-one even remembers you're there. Basically, stand next to Nebraska and keep schtum.

WOULDN'T IT BE EASIER FOR ME TO DISGUISE MYSELF AS NEW JERSEY? I MEAN, ALL I'D HAVE TO DO IS TIP THE CONTENTS OF MY TRASH CAN OVER MY HEAD AND THEN PLAY BRUCE SPRINGSTEEN TAPES REAL LOUD. PLUS I'D BE RIGHT NEXT TO NEW YORK, WHICH IS WHERE ALL THE ACTION IS...

Look, who's writing this book, O.K?

SORRY.

One word of warning. If you live with someone, please take them into consideration before choosing your new identity. If your partner doesn't know about your super identity, changing your lifestyle can be a dead giveaway! Even partners who know you're a superhero may not take too kindly to a violently drastic change...

A GOOD TRANSFORMATION:

HERO: Hi, Honey! I've become a millionaire playboy! Let's celebrate!

GIRLFRIEND: YIPPEE!

A BAD TRANSFORMATION:

WIFE: Oh My God!

HERO: Hssst! Honey, it's me!

WIFE: WHAT? I don't understand! Bob?

HERO: This is my new secret identity! What do you think?

WIFE: I...I...I

HERO: Well, do I look like Iowa or not?

WIFE: I...I...I...

HERO: I thought I'd become a State of the Union.

WIFE: Oh God, Bob. I knew your shape changing powers were crazy but...

HERO: Don't worry, Hon. I can still become Patrick Swayze on Friday Nights, hey hey hey!

WIFE: Bob, I just can't live this life! I can't pretend to be the wife of a state of the Union. People will...will think I'm crazy.

HERO: Captain Proteus is married...and he's Mount Rushmore...

WIFE: You're arable farmland, Bob! I can't love arable farmland! And we were planning to start a family! What are our children going to be? They're part of you, Bob! If you think I'm going to give birth to Des Moines, you're even crazier than I think you are!
    What am I going to say at dinner parties? 'Hi, this is my husband Bob: He's Iowa...?'

HERO: They don't have many dinner parties in Iowa...I'm rustic.

WIFE: Shut up! I can't take this! What am I supposed to do now? Throw away your picture in my purse and replace it with a Texaco map?

HERO: I'm a nice place to live...

WIFE: I don't care! Oh, God, what will the neighbors say?

HERO: Hey, that's OK. I know Missouri! It's Mr Changeling. He's a million laughs...

Note from Steve Dillon to M & M:

THANK YOU FROM THE BOTTOM OF MY HEART FOR NOT ASKING ME TO ILLUSTRATE THE ABOVE

ARE THERE ANY 'SECRET IDENTITIES' WHICH I SHOULD DEFINITELY AVOID?

Certainly. Whatever you do, avoid choosing one of the following:
➡ Another superhero
➡ A naval rating aboard a nuclear submarine that spends most of its time on patrol under the polar icecap
➡ A rather large, talking raccoon called Harold
➡ A rather large, talking raccoon called anything else
➡ Anyone who's dead
➡ A woman
➡ A supervillain
➡ The Andromeda Galaxy (If you go off to fight a supervillain, astronomers will notice you're missing)
➡ A specific portion of your own anatomy
➡ A known serial killer who's still on the run
➡ Anyone who's two feet shorter or sixty pounds heavier than you are

MY PARTNER DOESN'T KNOW I'M A SUPERHERO...AND I WANT TO KEEP IT THAT WAY. WHEN I'M IN MY SECRET IDENTITY, HOW CAN I SNEAK OUT TO FIGHT CRIME WITHOUT GIVING THE GAME AWAY?

Be warned now; she *will* find out eventually, no matter how careful you think you're being! Remember Janice? She knew somehow, didn't she...and when she finds out that you're secretly a superhero, she's liable to raise the roof!

HEY! BUT I DON'T KNOW NO JANICE...

We weren't talking to you, but as it happens, how long do you think it's going to be before *your* wife finds out about you and...

CHRIST GUYS, SHHHH! MY WIFE COULD PICK UP THIS BOOK...

Look, women are naturally suspicious – especially when you make a habit of sneaking back into the house at 2am, physically exhausted with your hair all ruffled, and covered in bruises and scratches. What's more, come back after fighting The Perfidious Perfume Princess or Lipstick Lass and the evidence is even more damning!

And what happens when she finds a pair of tights around the place that aren't hers, or the Avenging League of Superheroes call you up for a mission and then keep putting the phone down when your wife answers?
Take it from us, it's probably best to tell her you're a Superhero right now.

NOPE. SHE'D NEVER UNDERSTAND. JUST TELL ME WHAT EXCUSE TO MAKE TO GET OUT OF THE HOUSE

OK, if you insist. Safe exit lines include:

➡ 'I'm just going out to buy some Cherry Coke, darling!'

➡ 'I've got to take the dog for a walk.'

➡ 'Time for my jog!'

➡ 'Larry called; He's sick, so I said I'd take his shift.'

➡ 'I'll pick up a pizza tonight ... save cooking.'

➡ 'Just going for a beer with the boys.'

➡ 'I'm going to the office late night fancy-dress party as a superhero. How d'ya think I look?'

➡ 'What do you mean, "Where am I going?" I *always* go bowling on Wednesdays!'

➡ 'Omigod! I just remembered I called Australia from the office and left my phone off the hook!'

➡ 'Zzzzzzzzzzzzzzzzzzzz' (Pretend you're sleepwalking.)

Lines you should avoid include:

➡ 'I'm just going out to have sex with another woman.'

➡ 'I've got to take the armadillo for a walk.'

➡ 'I'm just going out to fight Quark, The Invincible Man.'

➡ 'Just dropping down to the corner newsstand to buy some stroke mags!'

➡ 'I'm going out to gamble our life savings in a poker game. Don't wait up.'

➡ 'What's it to you where I'm going, bitch?'

➡ 'Hell! I almost forgot my appointment at the venereologists!'

➡ 'God, I never realized before how truly ugly you are! This is goodbye, babe!'

➡ 'Gotta feed my secret heroin habit ... now!'

➡ 'I'm going out to join the Hare Krishnas. Won't be long.'

➡ 'It's the League of Superheroes, they've just called an emergency meeting on their orbiting space station. Gotta dash!'

➡ 'Going out? I'm not going out! I'm just coming in, walking backwards.'

➡ 'Jeez! Did you hear that siren? It's the three-minute warning. I knew we shouldn't have trusted that Gorbachov! I'll see you in the shelters!'

But she'll always find out what you're doing in the end.

SO THEY ALWAYS FIND OUT IN THE END, HUH? WHAT USUALLY GIVES US AWAY?

There are hundreds of little ways in which the person closest to you can tell you're really a superhero, but here are the ten most common ways in which your partner is likely to uncover your secret...

1. You park your Crimemobile in the garage.
2. You put your dirty costume in the laundry basket.
3. You keep shouting, 'Eat disintergrator blast, Crimemaster!' in your sleep.
4. You've been glowing in the dark for the past year.
5. She comes home early from nightschool to find you playing poker with Dr Robot and The Incredible Swamp Beast.
6. You go to give her a hug ... and all her vital organs shoot out through her ears.
7. Mrs Lipschwitz from next door saw you taking off on your way to Neptune last week.
8. Your new baby emits gamma rays.
9. You take four-fifteenths of a second to build the new summer house.
10. She is kidnapped by a supervillain and you have to rescue her. Inevitably – if she's got anything between her ears – she'll recognize you straight away...

GIRLFRIEND: Thanks for rescuing me, Squidman! Oh ... you're my boyfriend Peter!

YOU: No, I'm not!

GIRLFRIEND: Peter, it's me, Shari. Don't you recognize me?

YOU: Uh ... my name's Mortimer ... Mortimer Squid.

GIRLFRIEND: I know it's you, Peter! I'll prove it!

YOU: What?

GIRLFRIEND: Let me have a look at your buttocks. If you're Peter. you'll have a small heart-shaped birthmark...

YOU: Hey! What? No! No! Get off! Let go of my tights!

GIRLFRIEND: Why are you so touchy about me seeing your buttocks if you're not Peter, eh?

YOU: Uh ... I'm a Superhero. I don't show people my buttocks! I'll get thrown out of the Justice Brigade!

GIRLFRIEND: We'll talk about this at home later, Peter.

YOU: Er ... I'm going back to my secret undersea base now. Where I live. All the time. With um ... a mermaid called ... Sally. Sally ... Fish.

GIRLFRIEND: You ... bastard!

YOU: Shari ... Come back! Come back!

IS BEING A SUPERHERO LIKELY TO WRECK MY PERSONAL LIFE?

Unfortunately, the answer is yes. No matter how close you and your partner are, or how much she wants to share your 'other life', you can be sure that she just won't be able to come to terms with your new lifestyle.

This is the kind of reception you could be coming home to in about six months' time...

WIFE: Hello, darling. You're home late...

CAPTAIN MEGAWATT: Hi, honey.

WIFE: Oh, no! Whatever have you done to your costume this time?

CAPTAIN MEGAWATT: Oh, gee, honey, I'm sorry. You know how it is: I got slimed by Melchorr, The Beast From Beyond, but I'm OK, really I am...

WIFE: Well, what is it this time?

CAPTAIN MEGAWATT: I don't know; Alien Hell-Slime, I think...

WIFE: Does that need a pre-soak?

CAPTAIN MEGAWATT: What? Um ... how should I know?

WIFE: It looks like gravy...

CAPTAIN MEGAWATT: Of course it's not gravy!

WIFE: It looks like it. Could it be gravy?

CAPTAIN MEGAWATT: Beasts From Beyond do not spray gravy!

WIFE: It could be *alien* gravy. They must have it up there, don't they? Otherwise, what do they have with their meat and potatoes?

CAPTAIN MEGAWATT: How many times do I have to tell you! It's Alien Hell-Slime!!

WIFE: Well, if it looks like gravy, maybe it'll wash out like gravy...

CAPTAIN MEGAWATT: F●#%ing listen! It's not gravy! I have just fought a pitched battle to save Washington, DC, from the most dangerous space bastard in history! The President thanked me personally!

WIFE: The President? Oh, whatever must he have thought, with your costume in that state, all covered in gravy? I'm so ashamed! Take it off this instant! It's dripping on the shagpile ... It's all very well for you. You're on TV all the time, you get to meet the President, but who has to clean up after you? Next time, the least you could do is fight a monster that doesn't spray gravy everywhere! That's not too much to ask, is it? After all I do for you? I'll bet The Invisible Shield's wife doesn't clean up after him like I do!

CAPTAIN MEGAWATT; He's got an invisible shield, you silly bitch! His costume doesn't get touched...

WIFE: Well, couldn't you get one?

CAPTAIN MEGAWATT: The Titans of Olympus gave it to him personally! He's the favored of Zeus! I don't have that kinda clout! I'm not even in the same superteam as Hercules. What am I supposed to do, travel to Olympus, prostrate myself before Zeus's throne of utter majesty and cry, 'Please, Almighty Zeus, can I have a Shield of Invisibility because my wife hates washing my costume for me'? Jesus, I'd never be able to show my face at a Crossover, Crisis, Secret War or Contest of Champions ever again!

WIFE: Look, if you're not prepared to have a sensible discussion about this, you can wash your own goddam costume!!!

CAPTAIN MEGAWATT: Yeah, alright, goddam it, I will! I'll show you! (*PAUSE.*) Er ... Where does the washing powder go in the machine? And then what? I just press this button, do I?

THE COST OF CRIMEFIGHTING

HOW CAN I AFFORD ALL THE HI-TECH EQUIPMENT THAT THE MODERN CRIMEFIGHTER REQUIRES ?

Unless you're a millionaire playboy or an electronics genius funding himself with myriad brilliant patents, it's tough to find the truly astronomical sums of cash you need to equip yourself.

You could try stuffing envelopes from home or working overtime at the office whenever the opportunity arises – but then what time have you got left to fight crime? (Besides which, you'd need to stuff approximately 74 billion envelopes to even make a downpayment on a used Crimemobile.)

Most superheroes try to solve the problem by selling their adventures to the comic books. But be warned: today the competition is tough!

Back when costumed adventurers first hit the scene, in the heyday of the Pulps, there were so many magazines on the newsstands that *anyone* could get a job.

In those halcyon days anyone with even the most feeble power or gimmick, like a better-than-average sense of balance, a strong grip or even just a particularly crisp pair of tight jodhpurs could walk into an editor's office and walk out with a cheque and a two-year contract.

Just look at some of the losers who were making six-figure incomes back then...

FROM *AMAZING AVIATION EXPLOITS, 1927*

DOWNHILL DONOVAN OF
THE CATSKILL STATE PARKS' PATROL

FROM *THRILLING TALES OF THE TOBOGGAN, 1932*

STRUTTER CANE—
UNITED PLANETS STILT PATROL

FROM *AMAZING SCIENCE FICTION STILT ADVENTURES*, 1930

Masroor Ali—
The Cross-Eyed Swami

FROM *TALES OF HYPNOSIS AND MIND CONTROL*, 1932

MR.~YOYO

FROM *THRILLING YO-YO CRIME STORIES*, 1925

DIAL 'B' FOR 'BLINDMAN'!

FROM *SIGHTLESS DETECTIVE STORIES*, 1930

34: RARE AND COLLECTABLE PULP MAGAZINES

JUST IN!

* ELBOWS IN ACTION! #2 (M) $9.50
* SHIT YOURSELF ELEPHANT STORIES #4 (VG-NM) $18.00
* THRILLING TALES OF THE TOBOGGAN #1 (F) $4.25
* ASTOUNDING TALES OF PARALYSIS #7 (Cover missing) $3.50
* AMAZING STORIES OF POVERTY AND SUFFERING #10
  (Note: Contains Okies of Venus by Isaac Asimov!) (VG-NM) $34.99
* THRILLING ANCHOVY TALES #1
  (Note: Features From the Sea They Came! by H. Rider Haggard!) (F) $12.00
* FIGHTING SALAMI AT WAR! #5 (M) $14.70
* INCREDIBLE STORIES ABOUT SOMEONE CALLED LAWRENCE #1 (NM) $12.00
* AMAZING IF SHORT TALES OF TWERPS WHO FELL OFF WHILE WING WALKING #11 (NM)
  $13.99
* POLYVINYLCHLORIDE ACTION #1 (M) $125.00
* THRILLING CRIME TALES ABOUT PEOPLE WHOSE NAMES BEGIN WITH 'K' #2 (VG – NM)
  $29.99
* TWO FISTED SHEEPDOG ACTION! #3 (Poor) $7.00
* BLAZING KASHRUT STORIES!#4 (F) $13.99
* F@#$ING INCREDIBLE STORIES! #1 (NM) $75.00
* EVEN MORE F@#$ING INCREDIBLE THAN F@#%ING INCREDIBLE STORIES! #1 (M) $90.00
* STORIES SO F@#$ING INCREDIBLE YOUR BRAIN WON'T BE ABLE TO COPE WITH THEM
  THAT'S HOW INCREDIBLE THEY ARE! #1 (Mint – unopened) $145.00
* WEIRD SEPTIC TOE ADVENTURE #3 (M) $17.99
* THRILLING HANDSTAND MYSTERIES! #5
  (Note: Contains Across the Andes – Upside Down! by Mickey Spillaine!) (M) $90.00
* SEMI-NAKED WOMEN IN BONDAGE FOR NO OTHER REASON THAN TO SELL THIS
  MAGAZINE #3 (Poor) $39.99
* EXPLOSIVE EARWAX ACTION! #2 (stained – otherwise VG) $11.50
* COLORED FOLK DO THE DARNDEST THINGS #1 (Ripped in half) $2.99
* CRACK VEGETABLE WONDER STORIES #1 (NM) $14.50
* SPICY COMMUTER STORIES #2
  (Note: Contains Whipmasters of Lexington Avenue by E.R. Burroughs AND Love-Crazed Slimey
  Alien   Rapacious Pus-Oozing Octopeds of Grand Central Station by Otto Binder) (M) $17.99.
* REALLY SPICY TALES OF HANGING THE WASHING OUT #2 (F–NM) $340.00 (Note: Contains
  Pegged and Helpless! by E.R. Burroughs)
* REALLY WEIRD RACCOONS IN SPACE WONDER TALES #12 (M) $47.25
* ASTOUNDING SCIENCE FICTION TALES FROM THE OLD COUNTRY #5 (Note: Features The
  Star Cossacks are Coming! by Otto Binder) (NM) $29.99
* G-MEN ON ROLLERSKATES #5 (F) $31.00

YOU'RE RIGHT. THEY STINK! I'M GOING TO BE A FAR BETTER HERO! WHAT'S TO STOP ME GETTING MY OWN COMIC BOOK?

For a start, you must ask yourself, *will my adventures be acceptable to the Comics Code?* The Comics Code Authority monitors the adventures of superheroes to make sure they don't contain anything likely to corrupt young readers...

TYPICAL THINGS THE COMICS CODE WILL NOT STAND FOR:

1. Anyone calling himself Penis Man
2. Anyone who transforms himself into a superhero by yelling the magic words, 'Hey, kids, smoking is really good for you!'
3. Unnatural relationships with any member of the animal or plant kingdoms, no matter how integral to the plot
4. Superheroes who restrain foes by sitting on their faces and wriggling
5. Superheroes whose costumes are totally transparent
6. The use of domestic appliances for either self or mutual sexual gratification
7. Cross-dressing (unless absolutely vital to plot development)
8. Anything that entices impressionable readers to leap off tall buildings and expect anything other than being turned into a sidewalk pizza at the bottom

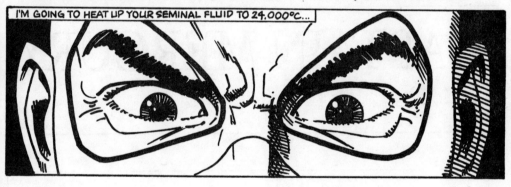

I'M GOING TO HEAT UP YOUR SEMINAL FLUID TO 24,000°C...

This man will *not* get his own Code-approved comic book...

WELL, THAT RULES ME OUT!

Don't despair! Many comic books today are published without the Comic Code's seal of approval, and those with more *risqué* powers are no longer automatically excluded (just tell them 'Howie' sent you). However, you still may not be able to get a comic book of your own simply because your adventures aren't suited to the comics format. This includes you, if you are a superhero who:

➡ battles injustice in 23 different dimensions simultaneously

➡ always attacks under a cloak of impenetrable darkness

➡ defeats your opponents by sitting in a corner and whistling

➡ wears a fluorescent or day-glo costume which requires expensive special inks

- is approximately 8,600 feet tall
- will certainly die if you ever resort to using your powers (e.g Mr Bee Sting and The Amazing Immolating Man)
- defeats crime by fissioning into ten million doppelgangers of yourself, all acting in unison.

OK, I'VE BEEN ACCEPTED FOR MY OWN COMIC BOOK!

That was quick.

I'VE GOT SUPERSPEED POWERS.

Have you checked the small print on your contract?

WHY?

Without a cast-iron contract, you may not have creative control over the way you're depicted in your own comic book ... Just imagine one of these on the cover of your very first issue:

CAPTAIN MERCURY™

He's todays biggest poison.

FIREFLY-MAN TM™

He's got all the Bee-Gees Albums

CAPTAIN POW

He likes young boys

Special GAY SEX issue!

I SEE WHAT YOU MEAN! WHAT SHOULD MY CONTRACT LOOK LIKE?

Something like this ...

---

10. The following do not form part of this agreement and are subject to separate negotiation: Royalties on future graphic novels & annuals; Serialization rights; Foreign editions and translation rights; Merchandising rights on toys, games, school stationery, slurpee cups, action figures, lunchboxes, decals, bubble gum cards and any other crap that manufacturers are prepared to pay a hefty royalty on.

11. The Publishers undertake to portray the Superhero to the best advantage and ensure that a square jaw, muscle-bound body, clear complexion, bulging pants and full head of hair are evident at all times. Actual imperfections such as the chronic overbite, large nose and weeping boils shall not be depicted in portraying the character.

12. The Publishers also agree to enhance the appearance of the Superhero's girlfriend whose bra size should be portrayed as no less than 48 Double D cup, so that the associates of the Superhero shall be jealous to the point of doing themselves actual physical injury.

13. It is agreed that no crap illustrators will be used and only those capable of depicting the Superhero's hardware and weaponary as the most technically advanced ever developed be considered.

14. The Publishers in consultation with the Superhero shall agree upon all storylines relating to the work and only those in which he triumphs over evil, usually against unbelievably bad odds, may be used.

15. The Publishers in consultation with the Superhero shall, if necessary, re-write storylines in order to ensure that the Superhero is portrayed as an heroic crimefighter and not a klutz.

16. The Publishers undertake that the following elements of the Superhero's origin story will be completely omitted from the first or subsequent issues of the work – the incontinence trouble, the six-month jail sentence for attempted corruption of a minor in Florida and the visit to 'the clinic'.

17. The Publishers undertake to indemnify the Superhero against any legal action resulting from purchasers of this comic attempting to imitate the actions of said Superhero, such as leaping 40 stories from a building yelling, 'I strike for justice!' and subsequently landing on their spines, or attempting to stop a speeding train with their faces.

If you get your own comic book, you'd better be prepared to start living with lies.

You know, and we know, that you can't always win: that sometimes Dr Nucleo is going to catch you in the scrotum with a lucky punch and escape with the takings of the First National Bank while you become re-acquainted with breakfast and wish you'd never been born.

Equally, sometimes a rampaging radioactive sea behemoth will manage to utterly destroy Boston because your wife was out with friends and you couldn't find a babysitter in time to take effective action...

In the world of comic books, the hero *always* wins. You'll be given credit for victories you don't deserve, and events will be grossly distorted to give you credit where you really deserve censure ... but you'll know the truth.

Can you really live with that?

SURE. I'M COMPLETELY SHAMELESS.

Oh, well, that's alright then.

WHAT REALLY HAPPENED

66

HOW THE COMIC PORTRAYED IT

WHAT REALLY HAPPENED

HOW THE COMIC PORTRAYED IT

WHAT REALLY HAPPENED

HOW THE COMIC PORTRAYED IT

I'VE HEARD THAT GETTING A COMIC BOOK IS JUST THE START OF MY EARNING POTENTIAL. THE REAL MONEY COMES FROM MERCHANDISING MY IMAGE. IS THAT RIGHT?

Absolutely! Selling manufacturers the right to use your likeness or name can be very lucrative, but, once again, the only problem is your conscience...

THAT'S NO PROBLEM, ESPECIALLY WHEN IT COMES TO COLD HARD CASH!

Look, when we were kids, toys were toys, right? Straightforward dressing-up costumes, construction kits or slot racers. That's because they used to make toys in the good old US of A!

Today, everything comes from Japan ... and they're different to us. What about *My Little Pony*? What altered perception actually thinks those day-glo abortions resemble ponies? Or 'He Man' – boy, are we talking major strangeness crawling up out of the Japanese subconscious or what?

We are delivering up the minds of our children to a nation for whom torture is a national pastime, committing suicide an art form, whale a delicacy and Tiffany a major pop star. Do you want to be a part of that?

LOOK, SKIP THE LECTURE. I NEED THE MONEY. HOW DO I GET MY SLICE OF THE PIE?

Just be very careful. Many careless superheroes have had their image plastered over all kinds of unbelievably unpleasant, strange or downright dangerous toys...

THE ANNIHILATOR™ INK TAG ($35.50)
Just like 'Laser Tag', but with indelible ink so no-one can be accused of cheating! Includes two Pump-Action scatter guns just like everyone's favourite vigilante killer uses – PLUS forty cartridges in red, green and orange and official 'Annihilator' badge and forage cap.

CAPTAIN MOUNT ST. HELENS™ PLAYSET ($43.99)
Exciting and dramatic toy volcano that you can wear as a hat! Will thrill and amaze any child! Features realistic 'lava' action. 4 x batteries and cooking fat not included.

'MR INFERNO'™ DRESSING-UP KIT ($34.99)
Look and act like your hero in this realistic dressing up set. Includes cape, mask, 1 x can of kerosene, 1 x box of matches.

'SUB-AQUA MAN'™ UNDERWATER FUN SET ($24.50)
With stick-on webbed skin and scales, shark 'communicator whistle' and tip sheet on how to hold your breath for more than fifteen minutes, anyone can explore the watery depths of nearby creeks and flooded gravel pits!

AQUA KING'S FISHYBOWL SUPABALL™ ($2.75)
An intriguing, highly bouncy play ball jam-packed with little fishes which you can bounce off walls, over houses, etc.!

CAPTAIN GIANT'S™ FUN STILTS ($58.90)
Extendable to an incredible **30 feet** high! Stride over walls, bungalows, cars, fast moving express trains, anything!

MR STRETCHY'S GAME OF VOMO!™ ($17.50)
The sensation sweeping through Europe has arrived here at last! Spin the wheel and twist yourself into odd and uncomfortable shapes until you puke! It's bad! For two to twenty players (if you've got enough disinfectant).

CAPTAIN EAGLE'S™ FLYING SET! ($62.50)
Fly just like Captain Eagle with this super mini-trampette! Measures 12" by 12". Simply position under bedroom window, run upstairs and jump out! Whee! Bounce as high as a house! Sturdy(ish).

CAPTAIN FELINE™ AND BLACKIE™ THE WONDER CAT™ KITTI-FUN™ PLAYSETS
Is your kitty cat just a wee bit dull? Now you can have adventures together just like Captain Feline and Blackie the Wonder Cat – with these super playsets from Kitti-Fun:

KITTI-FUN™ CAT SADDLE ($18.50)
(Not recommended for over-2's)

KITTI-FUN™ BARNSTORMING SET ($22.50)
(Everything you need to make an exciting aerial runway for your cat! Includes two Kitti-Clamps™)

KITTI-FUN™ FROGCAT ($16.50)
(Have bathtub adventures with your cat! Contains four flippers, weight belt, mini-mask and snorkel! Dive for sunken treasure! Explore the ocean depths. Will also work in rain barrel, pond or storm drain!)

KITTI-FUN™ 'CURSE OF THE MUMMY'S TOMB' ($16.50)
(Contains safe, non-toxic cat-sized cardboard pyramid and 40 feet of bandages!)

KITTI-FUN™ PUSSY PARATROOPER ($19.50)
(Contains camouflage jacket, rugged cat-sized protective helmet and handkerchief-sized parachute. Green light! Go! Go! Go!)

PRE-PUBESCENT IRRADIATED SUMO PORCUPINES™ ($9.90)
Your very own cuddly porcupine! Brush and style their quills – but be careful of their razor sharp points! Choose from four delightful little playmates: Slasher, Spiney, Ripper and Spike.

I'M UTTERLY SHAMELESS! I WANT TO MILK THOSE LITTLE DWEEBS FOR ALL THEIR ALLOWANCE MONEY UNTIL THEY SQUEAL! WHAT ELSE CAN I DO TO GET MY HANDS ON THEIR CASH?

You could consider setting up a fan club for yourself. Running a fan club is what they call 'easy money'. The principle is simple: make sure that the items offered to members don't cost more than cost $1.75 to produce; then charge at least $15 a year to join.

However, when you're in contact with children you have to appear whiter than white. These kids look up to you and are very easily influenced, so take extra special care to leave a good impression.

GOOD AND BAD THINGS TO OFFER IN YOUR FAN CLUB

GOOD	BAD
10" x 8" glossy color photo of yourself	10" x 8" glossy color photo of yourself – naked on a tigerskin rug
A plastic replica of your Power Ring	Your actual highly dangerous Power Ring, sent by mistake
A competition to meet you in person and have a personal tour around your crimecave	A competition to spend 48 hours with you and a few six-packs in a downtown motel
You, featured in a special anti-smoking anti-drug, and anti-drinking wall poster	Coupon for $2 off a six-pack of Bud
A wallchart to record all your battles and the supervillains defeated	A wallchart to record all the money you make from the sponsorship deals and product endorsements
A top-secret letter, written in code, with a decoder	A top-secret letter, written in code
A welcoming letter that begins 'Dear Loyal Fan'...	A welcoming letter that begins 'Dear Sucker'...
A cut-away diagram of your Crimemobile	A cut-away diagram of your Superpet

I GOT TURNED DOWN FOR A COMIC BOOK. HOW ELSE CAN I RAISE FUNDS?

• APPLY FOR A BANK LOAN.

Applying for a bank loan should only be considered as a last resort, not just because banks are gigantic, thieving, parasitic bloodsuckers but because to be considered for a loan you'll need to apply in your secret identity (they're not all that keen on masked men...)

SUPERHERO: Good morning. I want to apply for a loan.

BANK OFFICIAL: Certainly, sir. And what is your name?

SUPERHERO: Captain Whirlwind.

BANK OFFICIAL: Ah, a captain. Well, we offer preferential loans for veterans. What part of the forces did you serve in?

SUPERHERO: Er ... well ... I didn't ... I'm not actually a real Captain. It's ... um ... just my alias. I'm a superhero, you see.

BANK OFFICIAL: I see. Well, superhero or not, for legal reasons I'll need your real name.

SUPERHERO: I can't tell you that! You'll know my secret identity, and my success as a fearless crimefighter will be in jeopardy!

BANK OFFICIAL: I'm sorry, Mr Whirlwind...

SUPERHERO: That's 'Captain Whirlwind'. 'Mr Whirlwind' operates out of Boston.

BANK OFFICIAL: ... I'm sorry, Captain, but I must have your real name.

SUPERHERO: (*Reluctantly*) Kevin Kopecknik.

BANK OFFICIAL: And your address?

SUPERHERO: The Impenetrable Fortress of Crystal.

BANK OFFICIAL: The Impenetrable Fortress of Crystal?

SUPERHERO: Yes. The Impenetrable Fortress of Crystal ... Oh, alright, 1054 Wilmington Road, Edgewater.

BANK OFFICIAL: And what sum do you wish to borrow, Captain Whirlwind?

SUPERHERO: About nine and a half million dollars.

BANK OFFICIAL: F@#$ off.

• Seek Corporate Sponsorship

If you're *really* desperate for cash, and you don't mind looking like a walking (or flying) billboard, then being sponsored by a company is another potential way of raising money.

The amount you can make may vary considerably. Obviously, a corner deli won't pay as much as a multi-national corporation, but then what is expected of you will also differ.

PREPARE TO MEET YOUR DOOM, DREAD-MASTER!

For $25 and free sandwiches, the deli might expect you to tell a few jokes, juggle or sign autographs once or twice a week when business is slow (and exterminate rats, roaches and assorted pupae with your Death-Ray Glare when the health inspector's due). Whereas for $700,000, a large hamburger chain would expect you to give their logo prominence on your costume and contract you to appear in three TV commercials and to open eight new restaurants in a twelve-month period (and exterminate rats, roaches and assorted pupae with your Death-Ray Glare when the health inspector's due).

The trouble with corporate sponsorship is that large companies usually have your contract sewn up tighter than a duck's most private orifice – so much so that you usually can't even fart without their permission.

ADVANTAGES OF CORPORATE SPONSORSHIP

➡ You can make loads of money.

DISADVANTAGES OF CORPORATE SPONSORSHIP

➡ You find yourself in ideological torment, torn between the need to finance your struggle against evil and having to endorse products that are utter crap.

➡ Your costume has to feature their corporate colours, which usually happen to be lime green, orange or puce (or all three in hoops).

➡ The companies with the money for sponsorship are usually those cutting corners on safety and public hygiene. As their most visible spokesman, you may find your pitched battles against evil the scenes of mass demonstrations by outraged members of the public.

➡ They insist that you must always face the camera during a televised fight to maximize the exposure of their logo, despite this affecting your performance (and possibly leaving you wide open to a sneaky energy bolt where you don't want one...).

➡ You have to take the Chief Executive's kids for rides on your back (where they will invariably barf up over your head).

➡ You have to make an appearance at their annual sales convention, where drunken employees laugh at you, try to reach up and snatch off your mask, leap on your back shouting, 'Giddyup!' – and invariably barf up over your head.

➡ They insist that attending the opening of a new branch office in Iowa is more important than saving the Eastern Seaboard from an approaching 200-foot Seaweed Beast called Kelpo.

➡ For some inexplicable reason, the company's ad agency wants you to appear on prime-time television wearing just a mask and posing pouch and clutching a large papier mâché carrot.

➡ You might find yourself endorsing humiliating products, like *Captain Thunder's Haemorrhoid Ointment – Dissolves Even Piles of Steel!!*.

➡ They may want to – er – slightly alter your costume to give their precious product full exposure...

➡ They insist that you use their products in the fight against crime.
(This may be OK if they manufacture napalm, titanium plating or radar equipment, but it's not much use if they make children's clothing, toothpaste or sanitary napkins...)

➡ Some sponsors will insist that you mustn't kick or punch supervillains, because it sets a bad example to children.

• Apply for sponsorship from the Trump Corporation

Of course, the big drawback, if accepted, is that you'll have to call yourself something like Trump-Man, your Crimemobile will have to be known as the Trump Car and your accessories will be called the Trumptransmitter, the Trump-Omnidetector, the Trumpcrime Computer and you'll get to your subterranean Trump HQ via the Trump-Pole...

* Deliver newspapers in the neighborhood

Although superspeed means you can cycle around delivering papers to a whole town in the time it takes the average kid to deliver to one block, this is not without problems – like getting your cape caught in the spokes and accidentally taking out several homes with an over-enthusiastically thrown newspaper...

* Offer tourists sightseeing tours

Superheroes based in New York can make valuable spare cash taking tourists on flights around Liberty Island, the World Trade Center or the Empire State Building and undercut the regular helicopter rides.

Superheroes who don't have the power of flight are not so fortunate. Being seen giving Japanese tourists piggy-back rides at super speed through Central Park or along Broadway is not good for your credibility.

* Place begging advertisements in local newspapers

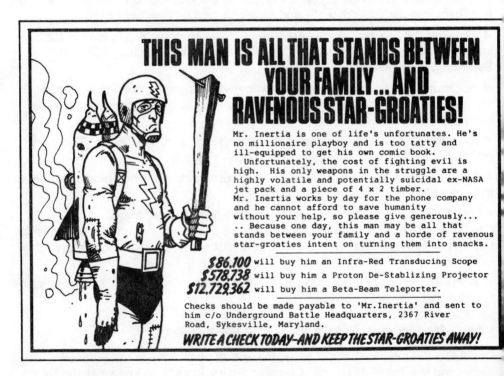

THIS MAN IS ALL THAT STANDS BETWEEN YOUR FAMILY... AND RAVENOUS STAR-GROATIES!

Mr. Inertia is one of life's unfortunates. He's no millionaire playboy and is too tatty and ill-equipped to get his own comic book.

Unfortunately, the cost of fighting evil is high. His only weapons in the struggle are a highly volatile and potentially suicidal ex-NASA jet pack and a piece of 4 x 2 timber. Mr. Inertia works by day for the phone company and he cannot afford to save humanity without your help, so please give generously...

.. Because one day, this man may be all that stands between your family and a horde of ravenous star-groaties intent on turning them into snacks.

$86,100 will buy him an Infra-Red Transducing Scope
$578,738 will buy him a Proton De-Stablizing Projector
$12,729,362 will buy him a Beta-Beam Teleporter.

Checks should be made payable to 'Mr.Inertia' and sent to him c/o Underground Battle Headquarters, 2367 River Road, Sykesville, Maryland.

WRITE A CHECK TODAY–AND KEEP THE STAR-GROATIES AWAY!

TOOLS OF THE TRADE

ACME
ANTI-GRAVITY
FLIGHT BELT

DO I NEED A PERMANENT HEADQUARTERS?

Every Superhero needs a proper secret base to work from.

Such secret bases are always known as Crimecaves. This is actually a misnomer, since only the richest of superheroes can afford to purchase and maintain giant caves, and superheroes of more moderate means will often have to make do with Crimesheds, Crimegarages, Crimetrailers, Crimetreehouses, Crimedens, Crimeattics, Crimebackbedrooms, Crimebroomcupboards or even Crimeouthouses.

The important thing about your headquarters is that its location is secret and that it's kept well stocked with crimefighting equipment...

Good and bad things to keep in your Crimecave:

GOOD:	BAD:
Robot Doubles	Rubber Women
Presidential Hot Line	Mickey Mouse or Garfield phone
Detailed map of the city	Color poster of New Kids on the Block
Crime library	Stash of stroke mags
Your Crimemobile on a turntable	Skateboard and ramp
Sick Bay and Auto-Medic Center	Tin of Band-Aids
Spare costumes	Basques and peep-hole bras for the rubber women
Computerized intruder-detection system linked to multiplex alarm	Piece of cotton stretched across the door tied to a small bell
Forensic analysis laboratory	Whisky still
City in a bottle, miniaturized by your arch enemy	Jar of candy
Teleportation tube	Bus timetable
Scale model of the galaxy showing all planets capable of supporting intelligent life	Model railroad layout
Trophy room displaying awards for crime fighting and body building	Trophy room displaying awards for bowling and cramming people into a VW Beetle
Computerized crime files on floppy disk	Collection of Anthrax albums
Secret emergency exit	Cat flap

Weapon calibration tester	Pinball machine
Gymnasium and fitness center	Fridge full of TV dinners, cold pizza and ice cream
Mainframe crime computer	Nintendo entertainment system
Hi-octane jet fuel storage for Crimemobile	Minibar stocked with Buds
Self-contained power generating system	Electricity meter and piles of loose change
Combat simulation area	Trivial Pursuit set

HOW DO I GET INTO MY CRIMECAVE?

Traditionally, access to your Crimecave should be by as exotic a method as possible...

Ideal methods of gaining access

- Sliding down a concealed brass pole with your name on it
- Standing flat against a bookcase which pivots around
- Holding your fingertips over an identification scanner
- Via a cunningly disguised trap door
- Making your way along secret passages built behind the walls
- Saying a secret codeword into a voice-activated door
- Stepping into a secret elevator
- Keying in a 20-digit numeric code

Less than ideal methods of gaining access

- Sliding down a concealed brass pole with someone else's name on it
- Sliding down a concealed giant scale replica of a penis
- Sliding down something covered in barbed wire and razor blades (whether concealed or not)
- Passing your buttocks over an identification scanner
- Saying 'Open Sesame'
- Keying in a 20,000-digit numeric code
- Kicking the door really hard
- Shooting off the lock

HOW CAN I STOP SUPERVILLAINS FROM INFILTRATING MY CRIMECAVE?

If you have the cash to run a proper Crimecave, then you also have the resources to build the most fabulous security system ever devised – a tortuous tunnel route into your Crimecave that's filled with perils, sundry unpleasantries and ideological minefields that only you can ever hope to negotiate successfully...

CRIMECAVE SECURITY PLAN

KEY

1. Crimecave front door (left ajar with a sign that says 'BACK IN 5 MINUTES'
2. Luxury foyer (shagpile carpets, cable TV, sauna, minibar etc.,) with sign board saying, 'CAPTAIN THUNDER WELCOMES ALL SUPERVILLAINS' to create a queasy sense of paranoia
3. 60-foot 2:1 sloping tunnel lined with large warning photographs of Pee Wee Herman
4. Signpost: LEFT: PAULA ABDUL SINGS 'OPPOSITES ATTRACT' WITH NOTHING ON
      RIGHT: EXCRUCIATING DEATH
5. Enticing hologram of Paula Abdul, naked apart from a discrete layer of fresh strawberry jelly concealing…
6. A pit of deadly spitting misanthropic cobras, driven into a frenzy by repetitive house music
7. Sign: ATTENTION SUPERVILLAINS. THIS LOG RIDE DOWN THE RAPIDS IS THE ONLY WAY TO MY INNER SANCTUM
8. White(ish) water (supplied by typical East German industrial town)
9. Razor sharp rocks and mutant 6-foot piranha fish
10. Genuine 19th-century French–Canadian saw mill with genuine 19th-century French–Canadian razor sharp buzzsaw
11. Realistic simulation of Hell with lifelike models of Satan, Jack the Ripper, Hitler, Ivan the Terrible, Cortés and piped elevator muzak
12. Hologram of Madonna, naked with legs akimbo, concealing...
13. Half-starved grizzly bear, securely tethered with string
14. Signpost: LEFT: THE SHORT CUT TO MY INNER SANCTUM
      RIGHT: LINGERING CASTRATION
15. Non-stop video-loop of Jim and Tammy Bakker
16. Dungeon of untold misery and depression (piped Leonard Cohen music)
17. Dungeon of untold crap (piped Tiffany music)
18. Hara-kiri swords with sign: FREE. PLEASE TRY ONE
19. Maze lined with mirrors – so totally baffling that 90% of supervillains would commit hara-kiri rather than bother to try to find their way out
20. Concealed pit containing something unprintable
21. Important looking sign in the extremely obscure Rigelian language to worry supervillains: 'Πœµ◊œ◊¬ Æ¿v¬∂åø¥ Ω∆¬¬°»'
22. Concealed pit containing 180 pit bull terriers and a poisonous plant
23. Chamber of K-Mart clothing (supervillians won't dare enter in case someone thinks they're browsing to buy...)
24. 40-foot slide out of the Crimecave – straight on to subway tracks
25. Irradiated 12-foot skunk from a broken home
26. Pictures of Nancy Reagan, naked, lining the floor, walls and ceiling for 120 foot (Run the gauntlet while all your senses rebel against you!)
27. 40-foot-deep pool concealing 39-foot-deep giant squid
28. Mini-cinema showing non-stop old Jerry Lewis movies
29. False door, with doorknob wired to subway third rail
30. Accurate representation of a party filled with accountants and mutual fund salesmen (guaranteed to have same effect as number 19)
31. To get through this part, supervillains must join a highly authentic Woolworth checkout line – and be prepared to wait for hours for service
32. Door with two holes in it and the sign:
      'HEY, SUPERVILLAIN! IF YOU STICK YOUR PECKER IN THE CORRECT HOLE, THE DOOR WILL OPEN GIVING YOU ACCESS TO MY INNER SANCTUM. CHOOSE THE WRONG ONE AND YOU'LL MEET (RATHER INTIMATELY) AN AWESOMELY VENEMOUS PARAGUAYAN PECKER-EATING SPIDER'
33. An awesomely venemous Paraguayan pecker-eating spider
34. Another awesomely venemous Paraguayan pecker-eating spider
35. Chamber of Narcolepsy (piped remixes of '70s disco hits)
36. 80-foot 1:2 slope upwards liberally coated with rhinoceros night emissions and broken glass
37. Warning sign:
      'DEAR SUPERVILLAIN. IF YOU'RE LOOKING FOR MY INNER SANCTUM IT'S THROUGH A DOOR ON THE OTHER SIDE OF MY SUPER-RHINO PEN. HE'S FEELING EXTRA HORNY TODAY SO I'D WATCH YOURSELF ... BEING JISMED TO DEATH ISN' A NICE WAY TO GO'
38. Super-rhino pen
39. Horny pet super-rhino
40. Door labelled: INNER SANCTUM THROUGH HERE
41. 200-foot slide lined with super-rhino number twos
42. Inner Sanctum

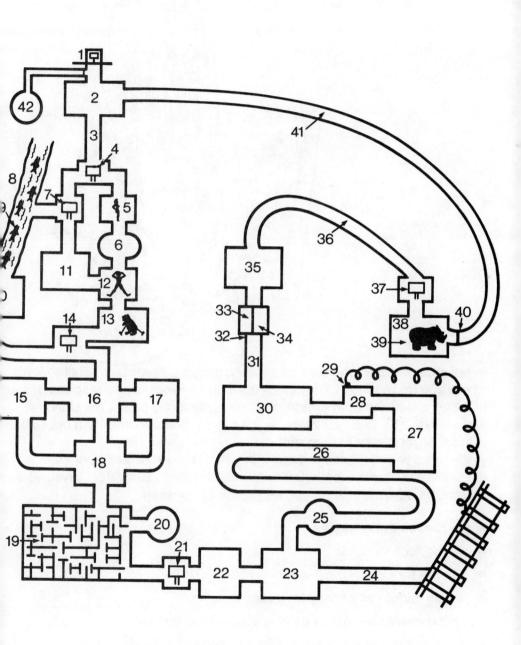

IF I'VE GOT A CRIMECAVE, THEN WHY DO I NEED A 'FORTRESS OF SOLITUDE'?

CAN WE HAVE OUR BALL BACK PLEASE, MR. INCREDIBLE?

Every superhero, at one time or another, needs a Fortress of Solitude. It's where you go to relax; to get away from all the worries and responsibilities of being a superhero; to ponder on those questions of life, the Universe and everything – and what's more, it's a great place to entertain hot babes without anyone ever finding out!

Whereas your Crimecave can be in your house, beneath it, or even in the backyard, Fortresses of Solitude must be miles away from civilization.

Here are some locations you might like to consider:

➡ In the Antarctic wastes

➡ In the Arctic wastes

➡ On the far side of the Moon

➡ In the middle of a rarely traversed desert

➡ In the desolate ruins of a yet undiscovered ancient city

➡ On a parallel world existing just one second behind our own

On the other hand, here are some you should clearly avoid:

➡ Slap-bang in the middle of suburbia

➡ In a busy shopping mall, with its location advertised on the store guide

➡ In the middle of Yankee Stadium

➡ On the Sun (unless you're 10,000°F Man)

➡ In the room you share with your kid brother

➡ New Jersey (it's miles away from civilization, but you wouldn't want to stay there)

OK, BUT WHAT SHOULD I HAVE INSIDE?

You might have inner doubts about facing Quarggo, the Indestructible Anti-Matter Being and your Fortress of Solitude is where you can confront those fears before you face him, bearing in mind that the fate of the world rests on your shoulders. That's why, among its sparse furnishings, a Fortress of Solitude should *always* have a toilet.

Apart from this, there isn't that much that a Fortress of Solitude needs. You're there to relax and contemplate,so you don't need all your worldly goods.

SO WHAT *SHOULDN'T* I HAVE INSIDE MY FORTRESS OF SOLITUDE?

Loads of people.

IS THERE ANYTHING ELSE I NEED?

Many superheroes find that a Robot Double is an invaluable way of preserving a secret identity. When they have to disappear on a mission, leaving a Robot Double in their place prevents any awkward questions being asked later. If you want to use one, be sure to obey these simple rules:

RULE ONE: Be sure to design your Robot Double to resemble yourself *exactly*.

Good things to have your robot double look like
– Yourself
– Your identical twin brother
– Your *other* identical twin brother

Bad things to have your robot double look like

– Anyone else, really

Study yourself thoroughly before constructing your Robot Double and don't be tempted to try and improve on yourself. If you whistle flat, have a flatulence complaint of almost supernatural proportions, pick your ears while watching the big game, stink, make women cross the street to avoid you, talk crap or usually walk around oblivious to something dangling from your nostril – so should your Robot Double!

RULE TWO: Be sure to program your Robot Double to behave exactly like you ... in all but one respect. It is vitally important to program him to say, 'Not tonight, honey. I have a headache,' whenever your partner makes amorous advances. Otherwise you could arrive home from an overnight stay on Neptune to find yourself with real problems...

GIRLFRIEND: Good morning, Dave. God, you were *fabulous* last night!

SUPERHERO: What? IN BED?

GIRLFRIEND: In bed ... on the floor in front of the fire ... in the bathtub ... on the stairs ... on top of the breakfast bar ... behind the couch ... in the attic ... on the porch ... in the rocking chair ... inside the closet ... under the bed ... what a night! Whooo!

SUPERHERO: Wha ... ? I thought I had a headache...

GIRLFRIEND: 27 times! I counted! 27 times!

SUPERHERO: THE BASTARD!

GIRLFRIEND: I guess all those visits to the therapists and letters to Dr Ruth are starting to pay off, huh?

SUPERHERO: It's not fair. He's got rechargeable plutonium power cells ... Bastard...

GIRLFRIEND: We just gotta do it all again tonight! Whoooo - yeah!

SUPERHERO: Er ... Not tonight, honey. I ... have a headache.

RULE THREE: Watch out for any early warning signs that your Robot Double may be malfunctioning. Warning signs include:

- Reliable reports of you walking down Main Street wearing a frogman's outfit and shouting, 'Restaurant!'

- Discovering the canary packed away in the cheese dish
- Arriving back from a mission to find eighteen trophies for breakdancing on the mantelpiece
- Father McGee asking you why you said, 'Kelloggs,' to him last Friday – 37,000 times in succession...
- The *National Enquirer* calling to find out if you're genuinely in love with the gas pump – or if it was just a one-night stand
- Finding your entire life savings have been spent on tartan socks
- Your best buddies wanting to know if you spent all Tuesday doing a handstand for a bet or for charity
- Your dog looking at you kinda funny
- Strange goings on in the office...

SUPERHERO: Good morning, Mr Mason.

MR MASON: Oh, my God! It's Bill Baxter! Call security! Call the cops!

SUPERHERO: What?

MR MASON: Is that security? ... Yes? .... He's back! ... What do you mean who? Him! Bill Baxter! The guy who just yesterday threw the Xerox machine out the window on to Mr Stein's Chevy, tried to fax Jacky Burnett from accounts through to the Idaho branch, head first, committed a possibly illegal sexual act with Mrs DeWitt's ear and then ran around the office screaming, 'Wrrrrrrrr ... DIE-PUNY-FLESHY-ONES ... Wrrrrrrrrr!' and brandishing the shredder above his head before running out down the street and headbutting his way through a police road block, that's who!

SUPERHERO: Oh, my God .... Wait! Mr Mason, I can explain...

MR MASON: Stay away from me, Baxter! You're insane!

SUPERHERO: No. No. You see, it wasn't me! It was my Robot Double. I'm secretly a superhero – Captain Jetstream – and I was on a vital mission to Neptune to defeat the massed Star Armada of the deadly Plutovian Salamander Men...

MR MASON: Oh, thank God! Here's security!

SECURITY GUARD: Okay, Baxter, y-you just stay right there and wait for the cops to arrive and I won't have to use this gun...

SUPERHERO: No, look, it's perfectly simple! I'll show you my costu... [BANG! BANG!] ... Wrrrrrrrrrrr ... show you my costume ... show you my costume ... wrrrrrrrrrrrr!

RULE FOUR: When not in use, don't stash your Robot Double away someplace stupid, like in your closet ... or worse, in your wife's closet...

WIFE: Now, shall I wear the blue or the ... aaaaaaaaghh!

SUPERHERO: What is it?

WIFE: I ... I ... You ... you're in my wardrobe ... I ... but you ... he looks dead...

SUPERHERO: Ah ... that's my ... er ... secret twin brother Leon. He's autistic and my family are ... ashamed of him, so we ... um ... take turns to hide him away in our ... spouse's closets. Yes, that's it.

WIFE: Your secret twin brother??!! In my closet? What are you...?

ROBOT DOUBLE: Wrrrrrrrrrrrrr ... Hi, Babs, honey! Wow, what a day I had in the office! I'm bushed! What's for dinner? Did you talk to George about getting the fence fixed? Where's Trish? Is she down the mall again? Kids these days! When I was her age...

SUPERHERO: Oh, God! Er ... ROBOT DOUBLE DEACTIVATE!

ROBOT DOUBLE: I ... Wrrrrrrrrr...

WIFE: Your autistic twin brother responds to 'Robot Double deactivate'?

SUPERHERO: He's got a rich internal fantasy life.

WIFE: We have to talk about this.

Follow these simple rules and you'll find your Robot Double is an ideal way of masking your disappearances!

ACCESSORY BELTS LOOK LIKE THEY WEIGH A TON! DO I HAVE TO RUN ABOUT AND FIGHT WITH SOMETHING THAT WEIGHTY SLUNG AROUND MY WAIST?

In combat you really do need to be prepared for *every* eventuality, and that's where a well-stocked Accessory Belt comes in! It may be bulky and cumbersome in a fight, but it's better than the other options available:

1. A Tupperware container
2. A handkerchief tied to a stick
3. A suitcase on castors
4. A cardboard box
5. A hollowed-out tree trunk
6. A *Mutant Ninja Turtles* lunch box
7. A picnic hamper
8. A supermarket shopping trolley
9. A purse
10. A marsupial's pouch (unless, of course, you're Captain Koala or The Amazing Mr Wallaby)

Good items to keep in your Accessory Belt

*   Anything likely to be useful in the fight against crime (you know, high-tensile nylon rope, infra-red epidiascope, mini forensic lab and clue analyser – all that sort of stuff)

Bad items to keep in your Accessory Belt

*   The one thing in the universe you're vulnerable to
*   A white flag
*   A pair of patent black stiletto shoes that, by coincidence, are exactly your size
*   A 'Doctor Death' fan club membership card
*   A note that starts off: *'If I am lost my mommy can be found at...'*
*   Anything likely to detonate if it's shaken
*   75lbs of granite
*   75lbs of anything else
*   A bar of half-melted chocolate
*   A piece of hairy string 2" long
*   A signed photo of Jordan, from *New Kids on the Block*
*   A map showing the location of all the public toilets downtown

I'VE HEARD THAT EVERY SELF-RESPECTING SUPERHERO SHOULD GET HIMSELF A NITRO-POWERED, RUBBER-BURNIN', HEAD-TURNIN', STREET-SMOKIN', BLACKTOP SCORCHIN', JUICED-UP RED-HOT BITCH OF A MUTHERIN' LEAD-SLED.

Pardon?

YOU KNOW, A FOUR-ON-THE FLOOR, BLOWN GASSER, ASS-KICKIN', HOT RODDIN', LOW-RIDIN', STREET FREEKIN' BODACIOUS CUSTOMIZED DETROIT MUSCLE MONSTER?

Er ... we're not quite sure what you mean exactly.

JEEZ! I'M TALKING ABOUT A CAR! WHAT'S THE BEST CAR FOR CATCHING CRIMINALS?

Oh ... a Crimemobile? You mean one of these...

KEY

1. PASSENGER EJECTOR SEAT
Useful for getting rid of supervillains who hijack you – or Boy Wonders who persistently pick their noses, pop zits or crack their gum on patrol.

2. RETRACTABLE LASER TORCH-CUTTING GEAR
Able to cut through 6" of solid steel. Used for clearing wreckage, gaining entry to supervillains' hideouts and getting out of parking lots after finding yourself accidentally locked in overnight.

3. RED LIGHT THING THAT MOVES FROM SIDE TO SIDE JUST LIKE THE ONE IN 'KNIGHTRIDER'
Not sure what it does but it looks cool.

4. HI-GAIN RADAR SYSTEM
Can track supervillains' vehicles, missiles in flight or spacecraft in orbit. (Can also pick up a 24-hour Danish satellite hard-porn channel to while away the time during a particularly monotonous stake-out.)

5. 600-WATT QUARTZ HALOGEN SEARCH/STROBE LIGHTS
Able to pierce even the densest of smoke screens. (Also great for discos, bar mitzvahs, Proms and giving oncoming drivers an epileptic fit at the wheel!)

6. TITANIUM STEEL 'NUDGE BAR'
Useful for moving obstructions and slow pedestrians.

7. REMOTE-CONTROL 'TIJUANA CREDIT CARD' GAS-SIPHONING DEVICE
For on-the-move emergency refuelling from other citizens' vehicles – since the average gas-guzzlin' Crimemobile only does half a mile to the gallon.

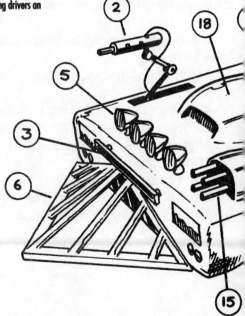

8. RETRACTABLE ELECTROMAGNETIC GRABBER
Useful for holding other cars still during on-the-move emergency refueling (see 7).

9. ROCKET-ASSISTED GRAPPLING HOOK
Handy for everything, from bringing runaway trains to a halt to rescuing cats from treetops.

10. REAR-FACING FLAME THROWER AND NAPALM SPREADER
Encourages pursuing supervillains to keep their distance.

11. RETRACTABLE SCYTHES
Watch those sparks fly during car-to-car combat. Also good for topiary in public parks or making forcible lane changes on busy freeways.

12. 300-DECIBEL KLAXON
Clears congested streets; adjustable volume from 'Please move over, I'm coming through' to 'Get the f#* out the way, dickwipe!'

13. HIGH-SECURITY PRISONER DETAINMENT COMPARTMENT
Keeps captured and trussed-up criminals under lock and key in this temporary ventilated cell. (Also ideal for keeping picnic hampers during Sunday drives in the country.)

14. AUTO-CAR DETECTION SENSOR
Used in conjunction with a hand-held controller — enables you to summon your car via remote control when you need it in an emergency (or when you've lost it somewhere in a busy mall parking lot).

15. FRONT-MOUNTED AUTO-LOADING QUAD 30mm ATOMIC CANNONS
Because actions speak louder than words.

16. REMOTE-CONTROLLED MAGNETIC MINE-LAYING DEVICE
To discourage pursuit by undesired vehicles.

17. GYROSCOPICALLY CONTROLLED AUTO-LEVELLING SUSPENSION AND RIDE MODULATOR
Constantly adjusted suspension adapts to suit the road conditions. Can cope with all surfaces, from 'freshly laid blacktop' to 'lunar landscape/typical New York street'.

18. MOTOR
Anything so beefy that it wouldn't look out of place in the boiler room of the USS *Nimitz*..

19. TIRES
Self-sealing, all-terrain type. Preferably four or more, but never less than three.

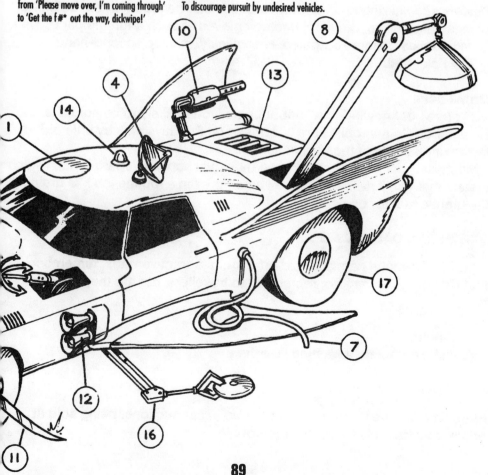

YEAH! WHERE CAN I GET ME ONE?

Try...

NEW CAR DEALERS

Having a Crimemobile franchise is becoming quite popular; dealers know that they're not going to sell many, but sticking one in a showroom is guaranteed to attract attention. Once browsers are in they can bolt the doors and concentrate on selling them the other lumps of tin on display.

Drawbacks:
– Most new car dealers won't understand, let alone be able to explain, the technology found in the Crimemobiles they stock (e.g. the comparative advantages of Hydrogen Gas Turbine and Proton Thrust propulsion.)
– Due to the high price levels ($800,000 upwards) their stock will be limited (usually to one vehicle, or maybe a glossy photo of one pinned to the wall).

USED-CAR DEALERS

Dealers specializing in used Crimemobiles can be found on the outskirts of most large cities. Since technology moves at such a furious pace, Crimemobiles become outdated very quickly, making second-hand models plentiful.

Drawbacks:
– If you're not knowledgeable about cars, you're likely to be sold a lemon. Remember, Crimemobiles are not driven on Sundays only by little old ladies or just to take the kids to school.
– Most used-car dealers don't have their own service departments, which means that you'll have to go elsewhere for even a routine job like draining the atomic reactor coolant.

EX-RENTAL CAR SALES

Although ex-rental cars are sold off at quite attractive rates, remember that Crimemobiles are not rented out to travellers, nor are they ever likely to be.

Drawbacks:
– You'll be completely wasting your time.

AUCTIONS

From time to time Crimemobiles crop up in car auctions, being sold at prices considerably below the market rate.

Drawbacks:
– Crimemobiles are usually sold 'as is'. Unless you know an 'Electron Flux Inducer' from 'Major Accident Damage' you'd best stay clear.
– The rarity of Crimemobiles at auctions means that invariably you find yourself bidding against every dealer in the hall, plus another 200 or so superheroes watching via mental projection, Supervision, Psyche-Omniscopes or through the eyes of their loyal ants and bidding by telepathy, astral projection and arms stretching half-way across the continent. It all gets a *bit* chaotic...

BUYING FROM OTHER SUPERHEROES

If you know the seller personally, then you'll have a pretty good idea of the Crimemobile's history. If not, then a few phone calls round the superhero fraternity will probably dig up enough details. Whatever you do, don't buy a used Crimemobile from Kamikaze Man, Son-Darr, the Somnambulant Speedster or some Robot Man who has shared illicit nights of passion with his Crimemobile – and spent every Saturday night for the last year pumping 10 cc of oil up the muffler.

Drawbacks:
– You won't get a warranty – something to consider when even a reconditioned Thermo-Deceleration Unit can cost up to $60,000.
- Bad feelings can occur if the Crimemobile goes wrong, sometimes leading to roof-top battles which can level a whole city.

IS IT ACCEPTABLE TO PUT BUMPER STICKERS ON MY CRIMEMOBILE?

It depends what they say! *I ❤ Iraq* or *I Brake For Jailbait* are out for a start, but the following are perfectly acceptable.

> I STOP FOR INNOCENT VICTIMS OF CRIME!

> HONK IF YOU HATE GALACTIKON, THE ANTI-MATTER BEAST!

> I ❤ SATURN

> EARTH – LOVE IT OR LEAVE IT!

> NO NUKES! (I'M VULNERABLE TO STRONTIUM 90)

CAN I REALLY PUT THE PEDAL TO THE METAL WHEN I'M IN MY CRIMEMOBILE?

Sure – but don't be surprised if you're suddenly waved down and stopped by the police because many unscrupulous drivers are now disguising their cars as Crimemobiles in an attempt to get away with speeding, illegal parking and all kinds of motoring offenses. That means that the police have to stop *all* suspect cars, even though this means inconveniencing those who are genuinely on their way to fight evil.

To prevent unnecessary delays, all you have to do when pulled over, is present a valid 'Superhero Driving Permit' to the officer. Go to your local Precinct and ask them to stamp the permits reproduced below...

Happy motoring!

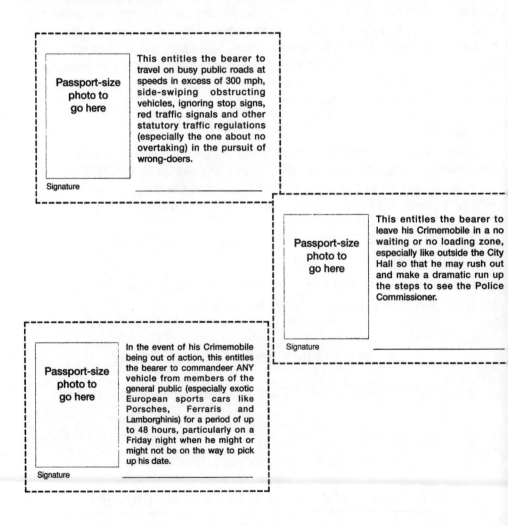

HOW DO I ARRANGE A DIRECT TELEPHONE LINE TO THE PRESIDENT?

Only the most revered and respected superheroes are permitted a telephone hotline straight to the President of the United States! It's a rare privilege you have to earn by constantly upholding the principles of truth, justice and the American way.

Once you are given such an honor, the President will always be on hand to take your call,at any time of the day or night.

Don't abuse his faith in you by using the hotline improperly.

PROPER USE OF THE PRESIDENTIAL HOTLINE

IMPROPER USE OF THE PRESIDENTIAL HOTLINE

Premeditated abuse of the Hotline, like the example shown above, is not the only way to lose this rare privilege. Accidental mis-dialing or ill-conceived pranks can also have dire consequences...

THE PROBLEM WITH BOY WONDERS

SOME SUPERHEROES LIKE TO WORK AS A TEAM WITH 'BOY WONDERS'. ARE BOY WONDERS A GOOD IDEA?

No.

RIGHT. FINE. WELL, I'LL JUST SKIP THIS SECTION OF THE BOOK THEN, SHALL I?

Wait! Perhaps that's too simplistic an answer. Boy Wonders do have *some* advantages, which we'll be examining over these pages and you really ought to be aware of the problems they can cause.

I BET I KNOW WHAT YOU'RE GOING TO SAY. YOU'RE GOING TO DO LOTS OF JOKES ABOUT HOW SUSPECT IT IS FOR A GROWN MAN TO BE RUNNING AROUND WITH A YOUNG BOY.

You peeked ahead...

NO, I DIDN'T. IT WAS BLINDINGLY OBVIOUS.

Well, sorry, but some readers might not have thought about it. If you really want to skip this section, be our guest. The rest of you, come with us.

Hey, there must be someone out there ... Anyone? Someone ask a question!

ER ... WHAT IS A BOY WONDER?

Thank you!
    Boy Wonders – those brightly colored bundles of energy and derring-do, always ready with a juvenile quip and merry banter in the thick of the fighting, forever by your side, eager to help and learn from you; feisty, bright-eyed, bushy-tailed, at that age when everything is new and exciting for a spunky little two-fisted scamp with the whole world at his feet!
    So, are they complete and utter dickwipes, or what?
    That's the common perception of Boy Wonders, but the truth is far more complex. Having a Boy Wonder to assist you in smashing crime can still be an asset ... if you can just find the *right* one.

OK, I CAN SEE THAT HAVING A PARTNER MIGHT BE A GOOD IDEA, BUT HOW DO I FIND A BOY WONDER?

There are a number of ways of going about recruiting a Boy Wonder...

This is the WRONG way.

And so is this....

This, however, is the ideal way of recruiting your Boy Wonder...

Of course, you can't rely on being called to the scene of a crime where a spunky young boy has just been orphaned ... but you *can* sneak into the local orphanage dormitory late at night and ask around.

CAPTAIN EAGLE: Hey, son. Son, wake up. Wake up.

KID#1: What ... Wh ... Wh ... WAAAAAAAAGGHHH!

CAPTAIN EAGLE: No,no,no. Shhhh! I'm not really a giant bird of prey! It's just my costume ... shhhhh!

KID#1: WAAAAAAAAAAAGGGGHHHH!

CAPTAIN EAGLE: Oh, well, you're a bit young anyway. Hey, son, are you awake?

KID#2: Yeah ... what ... Captain Eagle???

CAPTAIN EAGLE: That's right, son. Mind if I ask you a few questions?

KID#2: Er ... sure, Cap.

CAPTAIN EAGLE: Were your parents mercilessly slaughtered by an axe-wielding sociopath?

KID#2: WAAAAAAAAAAAAAAGGGGHHHHHH!

CAPTAIN EAGLE: Shhhh! Shhhhh! Is that a yes or a no?

KID#2: My parents ... sob ... sob ... they died in an automobile accident ... sob ... and it was all the manufacturer's fault! How I'd like to get even!

CAPTAIN EAGLE: Er ... just forget it, son. I'm not taking on any multi-national car company. Sh.., I wear a funny costume, but I'm not *that* crazy. Just go back to sleep now...

KID#1:WAAAAAAAAAAAAAAGGGGGHHHHH! There's a big bird in the room!

KID#2: Sob! Sob! Sob!

KID#3: What's going on?

KID#4: What's all the noise? What time is it?

CAPTAIN EAGLE: Er ... Hi, I'm Captain Eagle. Anyone here with parents who were mercilessly chopped into human french fries by some nutso axe freak?

KID#4: Jimmy Robinson...

CAPTAIN EAGLE: Great! Er ... I mean, how awful. Where is he?

KID#4: Captain Praying Mantis came by a few nights ago and recruited him to be *his* Boy Wonder.

CAPTAIN EAGLE: Sh..! Oh ... sorry, kids, sorry. Um ... you: how'd your parents bite the big one?

KID#3: WAAAAAAAAAAAAAGGGGGGHHHHH!

KID#1: WAAAAAAAAAAAAGGGHHHH! Big bird! Big bird!

KID#4: Er ... he don't like to be reminded, Cap.

KID#1: WAAAAAAAAAAAAGGGGHHH! I pooped my pants! I pooped my pants!

CAPTAIN EAGLE: OK, OK. Just everyone quieten down! Jeez, what a bunch of mother's boys...

KID#3: WAAAAAAAAAAAAAGGGGHHHHHHHHH! MOMMY!!!

CAPTAIN EAGLE: Oh, God! I'm sorry! I'm sorry! Look, let's just get one thing straight before I go any farther...

KID#3: WAAAAAAAAAAAAAGGGGHHHHHHHHH! DADDY!!!

CAPTAIN EAGLE: No ... No ... I said farther, as in further, not ... not whatever ... Look, just shut up all of you! Now, is there anyone here who has been orphaned by criminals and would like to help me fight crime?

KID#5: Me!

CAPTAIN EAGLE: Great! Come on, son! Let's away to the crimecave!

KID#4: But you've only got one leg, Bobby-Ray...

CAPTAIN EAGLE: WHAT?!!?

KID#5: So? I can out-hop anyone here!

CAPTAIN EAGLE: Er ... sorry, son, but crimefighting's not for unipeds. Best to stick to ... uh ... stick to ... er ... trying to stay upright or something!

KID#4: I'll come, Cap! My parents didn't get killed by crooks or nothing, but they had their car radio stolen one time...

(PAUSE)

CAPTAIN EAGLE: You're in!

HOW CAN MY BOY WONDER ASSIST ME ON MY CRUSADE AGAINST CRIME?

Sometimes team work is a more effective way of fighting crime than trying to go it alone. Take, for example, the case of Pogo-Man. Working solo, this superhero will encounter severe problems...

But with a Boy Wonder to back him up, he becomes a lethal force in the fight against crime...

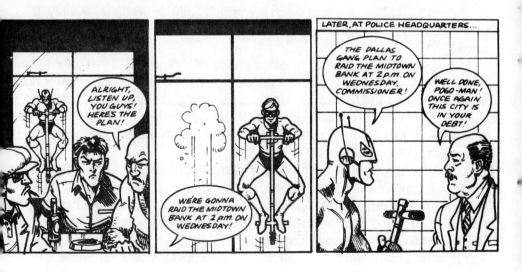

To be fair to them, Boy Wonders can help you in a number of ways. For example...

➡ They can watch your back in the thick of the fight

➡ They can carry your accessory belt if you're feeling lazy

➡ They're small and supple enough to be able to wriggle out of their bonds and free you from the Puffinmaster's diabolical death trap – just in time!

➡ They make you look taller and hunkier by comparison

➡ They're just about the right height for headbutting or biting a supervillain in the nuts – which makes them a force to be feared in the criminal underworld!

➡ They're someone you can explain the plot to for the benefit of particularly slow readers

➡ They can give your comic a vital sales boost – simply by getting themselves killed

➡ When they die, you have an excuse to go on a protracted frenzied rampage of violent revenge – and keep those sales figures high!

SO FAR BOY WONDERS DON'T SOUND SO BAD. WHAT'S THE PROBLEM?

The heyday of the Boy Wonder was really the 1940s – before the concept of the modern teenager had been invented. Today's youth is, frankly, far less suited to crimefighting – and far more suited to sweeping up at the local 7–11.

Today, you simply cannot trust your Boy Wonder. He'll lie to your face without thinking twice. He'll tell you things like 'I hear that Criminal King is planning to raid the 'Pulsating Hemorrhoids' gig tonight! We'd better be there in the front row to stop him!' or 'Holy Consumerism! I bet The Weasel is hiding out down at the mall! Let's head on down there and check everywhere out, especially the record shops!'

Worse, he'll swear blind that Candy Kapotchnik from his class is really the Muto-Time Master in disguise and insist that you both go and look in her bedroom window that night, or that Barry Pratt, the school bully, is really Gorgo the Star-Bomb and get you to call out the entire Justice Brigade of Superheroes to fight him.

It is statistically highly unlikely that any of his teachers are really 'Neptunian shapeshifting infiltrators that need dumping back on their home planet before they can do any real harm, like before tomorrow's history test, for example' – but that's what he'll tell you.

Turn your back on him for a second and he'll have ripped off the hubcaps from your Crimemobile and sold them for beer money, ripped his expensive new costume to rags 'because it looks real cool that way' or released your arch enemy, Doctor Psycho, in exchange for two front row tickets at next week's Satan's Spaniel-Buggerers' gig.

And if that makes keeping a Boy Wonder look like a full-time job, just consider these other little problems that come with the territory...

➡ They'd much rather stay in and play *Nintendo* than go out on patrol with you

➡ They get shy and awkward when confronted by a female supervillain

➡ They pick their noses when you're with the Police Commissioner

➡ They understand how the Crimecomputer works far better than you do

➡ They want to wear a Walkman into combat.

➡ People talk...

➡ A 13-year-old boy is no match for a 210-lb criminal sociopath with a death-ray glare

➡ They go into a sulk if you won't play a twelve-day game of Dungeons and Dragons with them

➡ They embarrass you by whistling at girls out of the Crimemobile

➡ They never tidy up after themselves in the Crimecave, so the whole place quickly gets littered up with dirty T-shirts, comics, skateboards, apes, discarded bubble gum, catcher's mitts, smelly socks, half-eaten candy bars, half-finished model cars, long-forgotten packets of contraceptives bought in a moment of supreme bravado and over-optimism, dirty plates, albums out of their covers, trainers, stroke mags, tubes of acne cream and crumpled tissues

➡ They don't wash, so they smell

➡ They think it's real funny to suddenly cut the cheese in public

➡ They can easily be taunted by supervillains into bursting into tears and running off – simply by pointing and shouting, 'Virgin! Virgin! Look everybody, there's a virgin Boy Wonder over here!'

➡ They'll quite happily play stickball in the midst of $20 million worth of delicate criminology lab equipment

➡ They get carsick in the Crimemobile

➡ In the midst of battle, it's futile to yell, 'Battle maneuver 18, chum!' – because chances are they can't count up that high...

➡ They call you things like *The Big Enchillada* or *Super-Dude*

➡ They get zits and look real unsightly

- ➡ **They think your bald spot is hilarious**
- ➡ **They talk crap**
- ➡ **They make you feel *very* old...**
- ➡ **They have to go to school during the day, which means they can only fight crime at night or on weekends and vacations. Furthermore, if the boy is your legal ward, you'll no doubt soon be the recipient of notes such as these...**

GEORGE WASHINGTON HIGH SCHOOL

Dear Mr Rossi

I have been handed an essay written by your ward, Doug Dauntless, on the theme of 'How I spent my vacation'.

Apparently, he spent it on Neptune, fighting 'Tortoise Men'.

I earnestly suggest that you seek help for him forthwith from the relevant psychiatric or drug counselling agencies.

Yours sincerely

R. Wilkinson

Principal

LEOPOLD AND LOEB JUNIOR HIGH

Dear Mr Brown

I am alarmed by the physical condition of your ward, Tad Taylor. He is covered from head to toe in cuts and bruises and his arms are marked by what can only be rope burns.

When asked about this, he would only say that the two of you had 'got into some rough stuff last night'.

I feel it only fair to warn you that I have every intention of bringing Tad's case to the attention of the appropriate authorities immediately.

Yours sincerely

K. Judo.

Principal

FORGET IT! I DEFINITELY COULDN'T HANDLE ALL THAT ... BUT I'D STILL KINDA LIKE A PARTNER. GOT ANY SUGGESTIONS?

Wait a minute. Before you decide that the disadvantages of a Boy Wonder far outnumber the pluses, consider another option...
A *Girl* Wonder.

This is the ideal Girl Wonder...

The benefits of teaming up with a Girl Wonder are really pretty obvious...

➡ They look much better than a Boy Wonder

➡ People don't automatically assume that you're, you know, *that way...*

➡ Overall, they're much more intelligent and mature than boys of the same age

➡ People think you must be OK to be seen in the company of such a hot babe

➡ Supervillains get dead jealous of you

And you might get lucky.

But of course, this seemingly idyllic situation can have its down side as well...

➡ They can't keep a secret. Within twenty-four hours, they're on the phone to everyone in their address book shrieking, 'Guess what! You'll just die! I'm going to be Captain Power's Girl Wonder! Fer sure! An' guess what? He's rilly that famous millionaire playboy you see on TV –

105

Dickie Donaldson! Like, it was just such a surprise!
Like totally!
Etc., etc., etc., etc., etc., etc., etc., etc., etc., etc., etc,. etc., etc....'

➡ They're always holding slumber parties in the Crimecave

➡ One tiny zit and they're out of action for at least a fortnight

➡ They insist on having at least a dozen different costumes to wear (and then throwing out their entire wardrobe every season)

➡ They won't fight crime if David Lee Roth is on MTV

➡ They won't fight crime if they're waiting for a phone call

➡ Other Superheroes will try and steal her away from you...

➡ They kill people when they're premenstrual

➡ They jam up the Emergency Crime Hotline with incessant calls to Tammi, Samantha, Jo-Jo, Mindy, Mandi, Shelley, Bernice, Pam, Tina, Debbi, Danni, Lindi, Shari, Sandy, Candy, Crissy, the Berkowitz Twins – and Scott

➡ If you receive an emergency call at 2 a.m. and they've got their hair in rollers – forget it!

➡ They're no use for fighting Tarantula Man or the Mouse Master

➡ Their approach to fighting Supervillains tends to be strictly limited to pulling his hair, slapping his face or hitting him with a shoe

➡ They get crushes on your arch enemy because 'He's like so totally dark an' mysterious an' mean an' moody – but that's only 'cause someone musta rilly hurt him bad one time. I can tell. Etc., etc., etc., etc.'

➡ They won't watch your back in combat if you've failed to notice their new hair style

➡ They get upset if you and your arch enemy start shouting at each other during battle

And, of course, if you chose your Girl Wonder purely on the basis of *looks*, you may not end up with the brightest of partners...

SUPPOSING I DO DECIDE I NEED A PARTNER, WHERE WILL THEY LIVE?

Taking in your Boy (or Girl) Wonder is no problem as long as you live alone (and no one calls the police), but how do you introduce this newcomer into your home, if you live with a wife or girlfriend?

Frankly, the situation is a nightmare.

You could always avoid the problem, of course, by renting them an apartment of their own in the neighborhood – but how will your loved one feel when she discovers (and she will) the receipt showing that you've set up a 13-year-old boy in an apartment close by?

It's also easier to respond to emergency calls if your Boy Wonder lives with you, so it's desirable that you get him into the house somehow.

You can't just smuggle him home and then stash him in your closet or under the bed or up in the attic and feed him on occasional scraps pilfered from the table, so you'll just have to be open about it ... and lie for all you're worth...

You could try one of the following gambits:

108

But, whatever you do, don't say:

BOY? WHAT BOY? I CAN'T SEE ANY BOY!

WE'RE IN LOVE!

HE'S GOING TO BE MY BOY WONDER AND WE'RE GOING TO FIGHT SUPERVILLAINS TOGETHER.

HE JUST FOLLOWED ME HOME. CAN WE KEEP HIM? HUH? CAN WE KEEP HIM—HE'S MY LOVE SLAVE.

SURPRISE HAPPY BIRTHDAY, DARLING!

HE'S MY LONG-LOST COUSIN FROM NEPTUNE.

I THOUGHT IT'D GIVE THE NEIGHBORS SOMETHING TO TALK ABOUT... HE MIGHT LOOK LIKE A BOY BUT BENEATH THAT JUVENILE EXTERIOR HE'S EVERY BIT A MAN!

HE'S MY LOVE CHILD FROM AN EXTRA-MARITAL AFFAIR, SO I'M RESPONSIBLE FOR HIM.

Introducing a Girl Wonder can be even harder. We asked two superheroes to try introducing a Girl Wonder into their homes. Here's what happened:

EXPERIMENT ONE:

CAPTAIN POWER: Darling, this is Barbi. I've decided to adopt her.

WIFE: Like hell! You get that tarty little bitch out of this house right now! Do you hear me?

CAPTAIN POWER: Er ... Yes, dear.

EXPERIMENT TWO:

MR INCREDIBLE: Darl...

WIFE: No!

MR INCREDIBLE: I...

WIFE: I said no!

MR INCREDIBLE: Oh ... She...

WIFE: Dennis! No.

MR INCREDIBLE: Oh ... alright, dear.

And even if you do succeed in getting your Boy Wonder through the front door, how long will it be before the little dweeb gives away your secret identity in front of your partner?
   Twenty seconds? Thirty maybe?

WIFE: I'm sorry, Sam, but I don't want a stranger in our house.

BOY WONDER: Holy matrimony, Thunderman! I don't think she likes me!

WIFE: He called you Thunderman!

BOY WONDER: Holy Slip of the Tongue, Thun ... Mr Simpson!

WIFE: What have you been getting up to behind my back?

BOY WONDER: Holy Giving Away Your Secret Identity By Mistake!

THUNDERMAN: Shut up, you little prick!

BOY WONDER: Holy Unexpected Bad Language!

THUNDERMAN: Nothing, dear. Don't be ridiculous!

WIFE: Are you being a superhero when my back is turned? Is that it?

THUNDERMAN: Of course not, dear...

BOY WONDER: Holy Smooth Talking Thunderman!

THUNDERMAN: SHUT UP!

BOY WONDER: Ooooooh! Holy Unexpected Elbow in the Groin....

WHAT YOU'RE REALLY TRYING TO TELL ME IS THAT I SHOULDN'T HAVE A BOY WONDER AT ALL. THAT'S RIGHT, ISN'T IT?

Right.

SO I COULD HAVE SKIPPED THIS SECTION AFTER ALL?

Yes.

THANKS A BUNCH.

TRUTH, JUSTICE AND THE AMERICAN WAY

I'VE GOT THE POWERS, THE COSTUME, THE EQUIPMENT AND THE BOY WONDER IF I WANT ONE. SURELY I MUST BE READY NOW!

Wait! Before you rush off into combat, you must first examine your motives. Why are you doing this? Why become a superhero?

THAT'S EASY. I'M A REPRESSED HOMOSEXUAL ATTEMPTING TO FIT INTO PREDEFINED SOCIETAL NORMS, REINFORCING MY OWN REPRESSIVE TENDENCIES BY ACTING OUT A STEREOTYPICAL MACHO ROLE-PLAYING POWER FANTASY DESIGNED TO SLOT HUMAN BEINGS INTO AGE-OLD MYTH PATTERNS WHICH ARE, IN REALITY, NOTHING MORE THAN CODES OF BEHAVIOR ASSIGNING AND REINFORCING GENDER ROLES.

Oh. Oh, OK. Fine. Jesus, we were just going to say that you probably wanted to fight crime. That seems a bit ... facile now.

WELL, I WANT TO FIGHT CRIME!

Good...

BUT I HAVE SOME DOUBTS ABOUT MY GENDER IDENTITY TOO, WHICH I'M HOPING THIS NEW CAREER WILL ASSUAGE.

Can we ignore the gender problem, please?

BUT IT'S CENTRAL TO UNDERSTANDING WHY PEOPLE BECOME SUPERHEROES.

Oh no, it's not. Superheroes want to fight crime. That's why they do it. Alright? Are you satisfied now? Fine! Now we've sorted that out, let's look at crime. First, what is crime?

The following are all crimes:
murder, assault, rape, arson, sodomy, theft, kidnapping, drug pushing.

The following are not:
crossing the road, taking a shower, eating breakfast, marital relations between consenting adults, marsupials, *The Price Is Right* (although it should be).

It's as simple as that.
   Our advice is that, you should specialize in stopping *all* crime, instead of specializing in dealing with just one type...

WOW! HE'S A CLASSIC CASE, IF EVER I SAW ONE!

YEAH! TALK ABOUT REPRESSED! POOR GUY!

Look, will you two stop talking to each other and let us go back to discussing crimefighting?

HEY ... AH ... WOULD YOU LIKE TO GO BOWLING SOME TIME? HAVE A FEW DRINKS MAYBE?

SURE. TUESDAY'S GOOD. THE WIFE'S GOT MACRAME.

Hey, will you please stop using this book as a dating service? Go and talk about it at the front of the book if you have to.

SURE. MEET YOU IN THE PRELIMS, FRANK...

Right, so you should fight all types of crime instead of concentrating on one type. However, be a little selective – think how stupid you'll look fighting minor offenses or transgressions:

BUT THERE'S MORE TO BEING A SUPERHERO THAN JUST FIGHTING CRIME, RIGHT? SUPERHEROES REPRESENT THE EMBODIMENT OF THE PHILOSOPHY OF 'TRUTH, JUSTICE AND THE AMERICAN WAY'. I'D LOVE TO STAND FOR THOSE IDEALS WHILE I'M SMASHING CRIME, BUT I'M NOT SURE I WANT TO BE A TYPICAL ALL-AMERICAN HERO...

Oliver North, General Custer, Mr T, Elvis Presley, Spuds Mackenzie, Ronald McDonald, Scooby-Doo and Rambo: yes, the list of All-American Heroes to date is admittedly less than inspiring, but that doesn't mean you can't represent the dream – if you're prepared to work at it!

HOW CAN I LIVE UP TO BEING A HERO?

To be a hero you must behave like one at all times. Never ignore a cry of distress just because your dinner will get cold, or let a rampaging supervillain go unchecked because it's raining outside. There is no such thing as a part-time hero. Whenever the call comes – if you're on the phone, on the job or on the can – you must race off immediately to save the day. (Within reason – no one likes to be rescued by someone with his pants still round his ankles.)

And it's equally important that the public perceive you as a hero. Never, ever, do anything which might tarnish your image in their eyes.

Here are a few simple guidelines:

1. DON'T RUN AWAY FROM DANGER MAKING LITTLE SHRIEKING NOISES.

2. NEVER SPIT ON THE SIDEWALK.

3. DON'T SPEAK TO THE TABLOID PRESS – EVER!

The tabloids are totally incapable of reporting anything you tell them accurately and will invariably misquote you. For example:

This is what you tell them	This is what they print
I STOPPED DR ANDROID FROM DOWNING AIRFORCE ONE AND SEIZING THE PRESIDENT!	I AM CHER'S LOVE CHILD, CLAIMS CAP POWER!
I RESCUED TEN PEOPLE FROM A BLAZING BUILDING	CAPTAIN POWER IN KINKY 'PUBIC TOPIARY' SCANDAL!
MR TERRIFIC AND I CAPTURED WHOLE BRIGADE OF SUPERVILLAINS IN MANHATTAN YESTERDAY	MARTIAN SPACE ALIENS THEY ATE MY CAR, SAYS CAP POWER
MARTIAN SPACE ALIENS ATE MY CAR	MADONNA BROKE MY HEART, SOBS CAP POWER!

4. DON'T LEND YOUR NAME TO UNPOPULAR PRESSURE GROUPS OR LOBBIES.

E.g. Pro-Animal Vivisection; Pro-Lowering the Age of Consent to Five (Four for Blonde Girls); Pro-the Reintroduction of Flares; Pro-the Reintroduction of Slavery; Pro-Sun Yat Moon's One World Crusade; Pro-Compulsory Nudity for all Women Over 72 (yuk!).

5. INSTEAD, DONATE YOUR SPARE TIME TO HELPING POPULAR CAUSES.

E.g. The Campaign to Drop Something Heavy on Dan Quayle's Head from a Great Height...

6. NEVER ACCIDENTALLY KILL THE PRESIDENT. PEOPLE HAVE LONG MEMORIES.

7. SUPERHEROES SHOULD NOT USE THEIR POWERS TO SHOW OFF AND MAKE ORDINARY PEOPLE RESENT THEM...

There is a great temptation, because you have superhuman powers, to consider yourself superior to ordinary folk. *Superhero arrogance* can be a major problem. Take the cases of Dr Psyche and The Golden Eagle...

PRESENTER: Thanks, Trina! Isn't she beautiful, folks? And the final contestant on 'El Dorado' tonight is ... well, a bit of a celebrity. He's a Superhero and he comes from Portland, Oregon. Please welcome ... *Dr Psyche!*

(Round of applause from audience)

DR PSYCHE: Hi, Larry!

PRESENTER: Hi, Doc. Can I call you Doc? Well, hey, what's the use in callin' you, Doc? You'll only tell me to take two aspirin and then charge me fifty bucks, right? Ha ha ha ha ha! Just kiddin'! But seriously, Doc, I see here you got some interesting hobbies.

DR PSYCHE: Yes, in my spare time I use my incredible mental powers to

117

foil alien invasions and predict where supervillains will strike in the future, things like that...

PRESENTER: Really? Hey, well, I'm sure everyone in our studio audience tonight would love to know who's going to win the 2.30 at Belmont tomorrow. Ha ha ha ha ha! Just kiddin'!

DR PSYCHE: Midnight Sun, by four furlongs from Sheherezade.

PRESENTER: Er ... right ... um. Well, on with tonight's show. Everyone ready? Fingers on the buzzers? Right. First question. What...

BZZZZZZZZZZZ

PRESENTER: Dr Psyche?

DR PSYCHE: The Maple Leaf; Pennsylvania; four funnels; ice hockey; David Letterman; a wombat; Andrew Jackson; five; Queen Elizabeth 1st of England; a papal bull; Stephen Spielberg; cobalt; Bernstein and Woodward; cherubim; false; Alaska; John Wayne; the femur; William Shakespeare; the moon; Atlantic Ocean; and black!

PRESENTER: What???

DR PSYCHE: Those are the answers to all the questions you're going to ask, Larry! And the six answers to win the 'Alphabet Gold Run' are: Sean Connery; 'Pink Cadillac'; Cortés; corpuscles; Al Capone and Capitol Hill!

PRESENTER: What????

DR PSYCHE: I'll take the Winnebago ... And I'll definitely come back next week!

PRESENTER: No, you won't, you son of a bitch!

DR PSYCHE: Hey, Larry, you forget I can read minds too. Are your wife and two children watching this show? Do they know about you and that young...

PRESENTER: Hey, folks! A big hand for our new reigning champion, Dr Psyche!

DR PSYCHE: I *knew* you'd see it that way...

It's just another day at JFK international airport...

TWA REGRET TO ANNOUNCE THAT FLIGHT TW312 TO ST LOUIS IS DELAYED FOR TEN HOURS...

KNOCK KNOCK

8. DON'T BE REMOTE FROM THE PUBLIC. IT MAKES THEM NERVOUS OF YOU. TAKE EVERY OPPORTUNITY TO APPEAR ON TELEVISION TO ALLAY THEIR FEARS AND SHOW THAT YOU'RE JUST A NORMAL JOE WHO JUST HAPPENS TO HAVE SUPERPOWERS.

If you're not used to appearing on TV, it can seem very daunting ... and can even prove disastrous. So be sure to follow these simple rules:

RULE 1.
Before appearing on TV, check your appearance out in the mirror. You will always discover a bit of broccoli wedged in your teeth – even if you've never eaten broccoli in your entire life.

RULE 2.
Do relaxation exercises to help calm you down before the show – otherwise you could end up barfing over the presenter – and not getting invited back next season!

RULE 3.
In interviews, don't use the word 'clitoris'. It is unneccesary.

RULE 4.
Don't get squiffy in the Green Room (otherwise you'll find yourself involuntarily breaking rules 2 and 3).

RULE 5.

Think carefully before you respond to questions...

INTERVIEWER: Good evening, America. My guest tonight is none other than the mysterious Captain Combat. Good evening, Captain.

CAPTAIN COMBAT: Good evening, Nancy.

INTERVIEWER: Well, my first question is: do you have a secret identity?

CAPTAIN COMBAT: Sure I do! I'm really Jack Jabawoski of 1244 Ceder Street, Biddle, Montana ... Oh, sh@! Sh@! Sh@!

RULE 6.

Try not to appear too pompous or self-satisfied.

INTERVIEWER: And can you tell us what your particular superpower is, Mr Nightwarrior?

NIGHTWARRIOR: Certainly, Jessica: I'm one with the night.

INTERVIEWER: Could you elaborate on that?

NIGHTWARRIOR: What?

INTERVIEWER: What does 'being one with the night' entail?

NIGHTWARRIOR: Um ... well ... you know, like the night? Um ... well, I'm sort of 'one with it'. Like I'm ... like the opposite of being 'one with the day', I suppose, and sorta like being 'one with the twilight', only a bit later.

INTERVIEWER: Moving along: What exactly is it you do – when you're 'one with the night'?

NIGHTWARRIOR: I'm the silent and deadly avenger of the night, Jessica!

INTERVIEWER: Wait, wait, wait! You avenge the night? For what?

NIGHTWARRIOR: Well, no, no, obviously I don't avenge the night! I mean, no one's done anything to the night – like insulted it or murdered its family or anything – that I'm avenging. I'm of the night and I'm avenging! I'm the Dark Angel of Manhattan, you know! Try committing a crime on my turf, sister, and feel the wrath of the night!

INTERVIEWER: So you're the night's temper?

NIGHTWARRIOR: I'm its righteous anger!

INTERVIEWER: So you're one with the night's anger but not the whole of the night, just its angry bit...

NIGHTWARRIOR: No. I'm one with the night.

INTERVIEWER: Has a supervillain punched you in the head very hard recently?

NIGHTWARRIOR: Well, yeah ... but, I'm still the best there is at what I do...

INTERVIEWER: Which is what? I still don't understand.

NIGHTWARRIOR: Er ... being one with the night! I'm she-hot at it! You ask anyone. You say, 'Hey, who's best at being one with the night,' and nine'll get you ten they'll all say, 'Nightwarrior! That dude can really get down and be one with the night like no one else!'

INTERVIEWER: Can you ... er ... demonstrate being 'one with the night' for the benefit of the viewers at home?

NIGHTWARRIOR: Certainly!
(PAUSE)
INTERVIEWER: Er ... you're just hiding in a dark corner of the studio.

NIGHTWARRIOR: You can see me?

INTERVIEWER: We'll be back after this short message from our sponsors...

NIGHTWARRIOR: Bet you can't see me now!

9. IF YOU LICENSE YOUR IMAGE TO A BUBBLE GUM COMPANY, MAKE SURE TO CHECK EACH AND EVERY CARD BEFORE THEY'RE PRINTED FOR CARDS THAT PORTRAY YOU IN AN UNFAVORABLE LIGHT.

Card 23
WHOOPS! THERE GO THREE NUNS!

Card 61
BEATEN UP BY MIDGETS!

Card 43
ABOUT TO BE BUGGERED!

Card 47
CRAPPING HIS PANTS!

In an effort to maintain a high standard of behavior in active superheroes the International Confederation of the Superpowered and Associated Vigilanties have introduced a *Superheroes Charter*.

If you would like to subscribe to this code of conduct, fill out the declaration below and return it to the ICSAV, care of their satellite.

THE SUPERHERO'S CHARTER

1. We do not kill our opponents under any circumstances.

2. It is not permissible to knee villains in the groinal vicinity, nor to gouge their eyes. The ripping off of limbs during combat is likewise frowned upon.

3. We (and our duly appointed Boy Wonders) do not curb crawl in our Crimemobiles shouting out lewd or obscene suggestions at women passers-by (or men in tight pants).

4. Those of us with elastic or other stretching powers shall not abuse these powers to the detriment of 'regular guys' who would also like to get a look in with the chicks now and again.

5. Those of us with the power of flight shall, in all circumstances, land before answering the call of nature.

6. We may not accept tips or gratuities from members of the public whom we aid. Nor do we ask them for their telephone number or invite them into the nearest alley to 'properly express their gratitude'.

7. We do not use bad language, no matter how many times we are kicked in the groin, or arrive just too late to save a major conurbation from a Mutant Amphibian Menace from Beyond.

8. Those of us with Boy Wonder assistants shall at all times maintain a purely platonic relationship with them, no matter how slender, supple and baby-smooth their bodies.

9. Handcuffs and Lassos of Restraint shall at all times be used for crimefighting and not for purposes of self-gratification. Nipple rings and chains are likewise not a recognized method of restraining captives.

SIGNED..

WITNESSED..

DATED.....................................

GOING INTO BATTLE

RIGHT, I'VE GIRDED MY LOINS FOR BATTLE (I THINK – I
COULDN'T FIND 'GIRDING' IN MY DICTIONARY). NOW WHERE'S
THE ACTION?

The key to successful crimefighting is being in the right place at the right
time. If a superhero knows a crime is presently being committed, he can
race to the scene and catch the villain in the act. But how can you *know*
when a crime is being committed?

1. IF YOU HAVE SUPERSENSES, USE THEM!

Use every superpower at your disposal to detect when a crime is going
down somewhere in the vast metropolis.

SUPERVISION

Scan the city relentlessly for tell-tale signs of a crime in progress – car
chases, blazing shoot-outs or people running pell-mell down the middle of
the street (but don't get confused and fly off to mete out justice to the New
York Marathon!).

SUPERHEARING

While your eagle eyes are keeping a look out for trouble, don't neglect
your ears! (Otherwise they could get all clogged up with wax and grow
little hairs that look real unsightly.)
    Your ears are your second-best way of detecting crimes in progress or
being planned, so listen out for shattering glass, alarm bells, the plaintive
wail of police sirens, the rasping sound of some hoodlum stropping a
razor or tell-tale cries like 'You'll never take me alive, pig!', 'Stick 'em up!'
and 'Help! He has a knife and I am presently being serrated!'

SUPERSMELL

Supersmell is not a particularly effective way to detect crime. You may get
lucky: one day there may well be a gang of Rampaging Swamp Beasts in
town to rob the Second National Bank – and you'll know about it before
they even get off the Greyhound, but most clues are far more nebulous ...
that sudden waft mingling the stink of dripping sweat and the
unmistakable odor of restless bowels, for example – is that a desperate
criminal about to strike or just a Turkish short-order cook?. And that
stench of boiling raw sewage – is that Zarnaxx, the Mighty Effluent Beast
wading up the Hudson to bring terror and destuction to the city or Teddy
Kennedy delivering a speech? You see how tricky it is?

SUPERTASTE

Supertaste is virtually useless in detecting any crime other than poor restaurant hygiene, since very few, if any, supervillains will ever commit a crime or outrage in your mouth.

SUPERTOUCH

If it's that close, you already know about it.

SUPER-ESP

The sixth sense. Some superheroes are able to mysteriously *sense* crime. Some experience this strange phenomenon as a vague feeling of unease, while in others it manifests itself in a physical way, such as a twitching nose for trouble or an arm which literally acts as a dowsing rod for danger.

Others are not so lucky, like Mr Tornado, whose balls start to itch like crazy, or Dynamo Boy, who develops acute appendicitis and has to be rushed to hospital each time a crime occurs...

A few superheroes can learn about future crimes in their sleep, but dreams are notoriously unreliable for foretelling actual crimes. If we all believed what our dreams told us, we'd be forever watching out for a blonde female supervillain with a 44" bust wearing a skimpy white leather bikini two sizes too small who intends to bushwack us, tie us up and then walk up and down over our backs in stiletto shoes, telling us that we're 'naughty little boys' and we need some 'stiff correction'....

2. IF YOU DON'T HAVE SUPERSENSES, GET THE POLICE TO CALL YOU OUT WITH A PROMINENT SIGNAL IN THE SKY

Having your logo beamed into the sky and reflected off a cloud by the police is a great way of attracting your attention!

However, for this method of communication to succeed you've got to have a logo that's simple; whereas superheroes like Scorpion Man or CatMaster can easily identify their signals from a great distance, Mr Invisible, The Amazing Shapechanger and Cumulus Boy usually have severe problems, causing them to be late for fights, or sometimes to miss them altogether, while the NYPD has not officially been in touch with The Purple Helmet since the Mother's League for Decency got that Supreme Court ruling (although he often mistakenly answers police calls for Doc Hemisphere).

The other main drawback of this method, of course, is that it's crap in daylight.

SO I'M AT WORK, SURROUNDED BY COLLEAGUES, AND I SUDDENLY BECOME AWARE OF A SERIOUS CRIME, APOCALYPSE OR ALIEN INVASION TAKING PLACE ACROSS TOWN. HOW DO I MAKE A SUDDEN EXIT WITHOUT AROUSING SUSPICION?

USE YOUR SUPERPOWERS TO CREATE A DIVERSION ... AND THEN SLIP AWAY IN THE ENSUING CHAOS.

...BUT THEN AGAIN, ONLY IF YOUR SUPERPOWERS ENABLE YOU TO DO SO WITHOUT ATTRACTING *TOO* MUCH ATTENTION...

YEAH, BUT SUPPOSE I'M AT HOME. HOW DO I GET THE WIFE TO THROW ME OUT QUICK?

That's simplicity itself! Just say...
• 'I screwed your best friend today. Now what's for dinner?'
• 'Sure I remembered your birthday. Your present's in my underpants, doll!'
• 'Why should I buy you flowers when you're too sick to thank me properly?'
• 'Put this blonde wig on, will ya? I wanna pretend you're my secretary an' do it doggy-fashion!'
• 'What's the point of taking you to the movies? I can get a grope off you any time I want.'
• 'Why should I do the dishes? You cooked the food that got 'em dirty in the first place.'

OK, I'M OUTTA THERE! TIME TO STRIP FOR ACTION!

If you're well prepared, you should be able to don your costume and go into action within a matter of seconds. So make sure that your costume is *always* easily accessible and close to hand.

GOOD PLACES TO KEEP YOUR COSTUME
– Compressed in your secret ring, where it expands on contact with the air

- Under your day clothes
- In a briefcase which never leaves your side

BAD PLACES TO KEEP YOUR COSTUME
- On top of your day clothes
- In a pouch hung around your neck saying *'Superhero's Costume'*
- In a left-luggage locker at Grand Central Station
- Abroad
- In the pouch of a marsupial in San Diego zoo
- Up your @#%hole
- Up someone else's @#%hole
- In a box protected by a 12-foot reticulated python that doesn't know you all that well
- In one of the footlockers on board the USS *Nimitz*
- Under your hat
- Anywhere that you can't remember
- In a safe protected by a timelock that only opens once a month at 4.00 a.m.
- Hanging from a hook on the inside of your office door

WHERE CAN I CHANGE INTO MY COSTUME WITHOUT BEING SPOTTED?

If you've got the power of superspeed, then it's safe to change virtually anywhere, even office storerooms, because you'll just be a blur to the human eye. Superheroes not endowed with this particular power must be much more careful.

GOOD PLACES TO CHANGE INTO YOUR COSTUME

- Anywhere private or deserted, where you're unlikely to be discovered.

BAD PLACES TO CHANGE INTO YOUR COSTUME

- In the middle of Times Square on New Year's Eve
- In a store window
- The orchestra at Carnegie Hall during a show
- In the presence of impressionable minors
- On the subway
- In a mail box
- The office elevator at 5.01 on a Friday evening
- In an abandoned car about to be crushed into a 1-foot cube
- In line outside a movie theater
- In your boss's office during your annual appraisal

- Right in front of your previously unsuspecting wife or girlfriend
- In the players' dugout during a live televised baseball game

IT'S MY FIRST BATTLE, AND I REALLY WANT TO SHOW UP IN STYLE! WHAT DO YOU ADVISE?

Let's look at the many excellent modes of tranport available to you. Any one of these will do admirably.
• Screeching to a halt in a shiny black Crimemobile, belching flames!
• Swinging from a high-tensile nylon line!
• Taking whole city blocks in your gigantic stride!
• Hurtling through the air, propelled by your flight ring!
• Astride your superpet, a winged steed (invariably called Pegasus)!
• Appearing from nowhere – thanks to your amazing belt of teleportation!

Now let's look at some of the modes of transportation you should avoid if at all possible.

A BUGGY PULLED BY FOUR GERMAN SHEPHERDS
Too stupid for words

HITCH-HIKING TO THE SCENE OF THE CRIME
It's hard enough flagging down a passing motorist at the best of times, let alone wearing a mask and brandishing a Particle De-Moleculisor Gun. If you really have to hitch-hike, don't take a placard. After all, no one's going to stop if they know your intended destination is the HQ of 'Destructomek – the Planet Smasher'.

THE SUBWAY
More dangerous than fighting supervillains

A ROCKET-POWERED JOCK STRAP
Also more dangerous than fighting supervillains

A PIGGYBACK FROM AN OBLIGING PASSER-BY
Too difficult to find when you're racing against time.

SWINGING FROM VINES
There aren't too many vines left in town these days. The modern equivalent would be swinging from overhead power cables, which is really not advisable...

WALKING
If you have to walk into action, take long, determined strides, hold your head up high and look straight ahead – except, of course, when crossing a busy street.

Travelling this way is acceptable, whereas other variations of walking are not and can permanently damage your credibility. These include hopping, jumping with your ankles together, skipping, deliberately walking like a girl and doing the Egyptian sand dance. Moonwalking, while looking cool, takes forever, plus you can only travel backwards.

MY *MODUS OPERANDI* IS TO SEEK OUT CRIME BY PROWLING THE ROOFTOPS OF THE CITY! DO YOU HAVE ANY SPECIAL ADVICE FOR ME?

Picture the scene. It's 3.00 a.m. and the city is in a dark, deep slumber, blissfully unaware of the titanic struggle between the forces of good and evil about to erupt high above their heads!

You are there waiting. The appointed hour chimes as your arch enemy approaches... He is near. You can sense him – the embodiment of corruption and depravity. He flits silently from rooftop to rooftop until, at last, he turns a corner and sees you silhouetted against the full moon ... doing an impersonation of a teapot...

Get the picture?

Act like this and NO supervillain, however chicken-livered, will ever take you seriously again. In fact, you're just as likely to be mercilessly slain on the spot by other superheroes for bringing the profession into disrepute.

If you want to be taken seriously as a superhero, you must learn *exactly* the right pose to strike on rooftops. It's not that difficult.

1. THE 'I'M A TEA POT' POSE
2. THE 'IF I PRETEND TO BE A GORILLA, PERHAPS HE WON'T NOTICE ME' POSE
3. THE 'FLEET'S IN' POSE
4. THE ' KURT WALDHEIM' POSE
5. THE 'WHY ARE YOU DOING A HANDSTAND' POSE
6. THE 'CAUGHT SHORT' POSE
7. THE 'JOHNNY B. GOODE' POSE
8. THE 'PHYSICALLY IMPOSSIBLE' POSE
9. THE 'RICKY MOOSE, CHAMPION OF GOOD' POSE
10. THE 'I'M IN IMMINENT DANGER OF FALLING OF THIS ROOF TOP' POSE

**I'M HARDLY LIKELY TO DO TEAPOT IMPRESSIONS ON ROOFTOPS!
WHAT I WANT TO KNOW IS HOW TO REALLY INSPIRE FEAR INTO
THE HEARTS OF EVILDOERS BEFORE THE BATTLE COMMENCES!**

Skillful use of psychological intimidation is guaranteed to unsettle your
opponents and undermine their confidence.

The objective is to make them think: *Hell, maybe taking on this guy
wasn't such a good idea after all* before quickly making their excuses and
leaving the area (if not the planet).

At the very least, you should be able to unnerve them sufficiently to
make finishing them off a simpler task.

THINGS GUARANTEED TO STRIKE FEAR INTO THE HEARTS OF EVILDOERS

- The semblance of a giant bat
- Courage in the face of almost overwhelming odds
- A true heart that is pure and unafraid
- A fucking enormous laser disintegrater cannon
- Finding out that you've just killed Dr Indestructible in battle
- A surprise visit from the Internal Revenue Service
- Being mistaken for Boy George
- The emptying of a bucket of Ninja lobsters down their tights
- A threat to set up an impromptu showing of *Ishtar*
- A superhero aiming a genital-seeking missile directly at their crotch and
  saying, 'Go ahead, punk, make my day!'
- Finding out that their name's just been given to the *Reader's Digest*
  Priority Mailing Service
- Producing a briefcase and saying, 'Have you ever considered the
  benefits of mutual fund investments?'
- Threats to turn their bottoms into avocados by magic

Alternatively, you could use the covers of your own comic book to terrify
any potential future adversary...

He'll rip off your nuts and feed them to chipmunks

He's not bound by the comics code

He knows what your afraid of, then does it to you - in slow motio

He puts trees up evildoers' bottoms

And then again, if you *really* want to turn evildoers' knees to jelly, you could simply change your name to something like *The Castrator* and redesign your costume to look like this...

TO TELL YOU THE TRUTH, RIGHT NOW I'M A LITTLE SCARED OF GOING INTO COMBAT MYSELF. WHAT'S ... WHAT'S THE WORST THING THAT COULD POSSIBLY HAPPEN TO ME?

You don't want to know.

I WAS AFRAID YOU WERE GOING TO SAY THAT.

Look, most superheroes are afraid of being maimed in a certain very personal and intimate way, which we needn't go into here. You can take certain steps to avoid this happening...

Cut out this handy checklist, keep it with you and be sure to refer to it each time before you go into combat.

IMPORTANT!

GOOD THINGS TO STUFF DOWN YOUR TIGHTS PRIOR TO COMBAT:
1. Titanium steel plating
2. Electronic Groinal Defense Shield
3. Socks (they make a bigger bulge and intimidate sexually insecure supervillains)
4. Acid-Resistant Gonad Shroud
5. Asbestos fire-blanket
6. Electromagnetic Scrotal Force Field Generator
7. Love Blob Auto-Security Screen
8. Genital-Seeking Missile Repulsor Unit
9. Bulletproof Penile Shaft Armour
10. Your Girl Wonder's head
11. Your Girl Wonder's hands
12. All of the above, simultaneously

BAD THINGS TO STUFF DOWN YOUR TIGHTS PRIOR TO COMBAT
1. Glass jockstrap
2. Epileptic lobsters
3. Bear trap with a dodgy spring
4. Napalm
5. 5 lbs of wriggling cockroaches (except where this may intimidate supervillains)
6. 4 gallons of quick-drying cement
7. Your barbed wire collection
8. Your stuffed porcupine lucky mascot
9. Strawberry jam
10. Genital-Seeking Missile
11. Your head
12. Your Boy Wonder's head
13. A piece of modern sculpture consisting entirely of razor blades

I'VE BEEN DESPERATELY TRYING TO THINK OF A BATTLE CRY TO YELL AS I GO INTO COMBAT – BUT THE BEST I'VE BEEN ABLE TO COME UP WITH IS, 'HERE I COME!' CAN YOU HELP OUT?

Every superhero needs a battle cry – an exclamation that makes his adrenalin kick in and inspires him to great acts of bravery and heroism.

A good battle cry should be slightly aggressive, show that you're ready for action and, most important of all, inspire fear in the hearts of your enemies...

GOOD BATTLE CRIES

BAD BATTLE CRIES

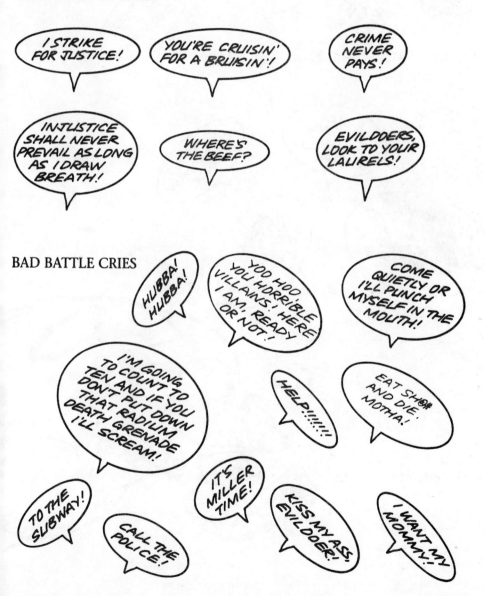

TACKLING YOUR FIRST SUPERVILLAIN

SO I'M ALL SET FOR MY FIRST BLOCKBUSTING BATTLE WITH A REAL LIFE SUPERVILLAIN – *AT LONG LAST*, I MIGHT ADD. WHICH SUPERPOWERED SCUMWAD SHOULD BE THE FIRST TO EAT KNUCKLE?

Since you're still a novice in the superhero game, in an ideal world you should tackle only easy opponents to start with,and leave the 'big boys' to superheroes with more experience.

Supervillains to tackle:

Fishpaste Sandwich Maker

Baron Scaredy-Cat
Fellatio Lass
The Crochet Master
Doc Won't Say 'Boo' to a Goose
Mr White Knuckles

Nosebleed Boy
Dr Scared Sh..less

Bondage Damsel
Sissy Man

Supervillains to avoid:

Emitorr, the Nuclear Radiation Man
Thargorr, the Planet Crusher
Fellatio Lad
Sun-Up, the Solar Sodomizer
Doc Slaughterhouse
Garth, the Gonad Detonator Supreme
Dr Disemboweller
The Slasher From Beyond the Stars
Krisparr, the Incinerator
Mr Rip-Your-Nuts-Off-And-Eat-Them-In-Front-Of-You

In real life, though, you must quickly decide which supervillain has the greatest chance of seizing power and becoming Master of the World with this ingenious and thoroughly diabolical masterplan, and attack *him*...

Supervillains who pose a serious threat will:
* Hold the world to ransom with an Omega Bomb
* Enlist the aid of merciless star mercenaries from the Andromeda Spiral
* Replace all the world leaders with obedient robot duplicates
* Paralyze the world in a Stasis Ray
* Seize control of America's tactical nuclear strike force by hacking into their computer system

Supervillains who don't pose much of a threat of becoming Master of the World will:
* Ask politely
* Run for head office in Papua New Guinea

* Find a steady job and hope to work their way up through the ranks to Master of the World
* Try to take over the world when there's nobody looking
* Tell everyone they're Master of the World – and hope folks believe them
* Threaten to have a temper tantrum until they get world power
* Make a cash offer for the world
* Disguise themselves as Master of the World – and hope everyone will fall for it
* Attempt to win it in a lottery
* Disguise themselves as Jackie Mason

But before you go chasing off to save the world, let's quickly review some of the different types of supervillain you're likely to come up against and learn how to defeat them.

NINJAS

Ninjas are hired assassins and masters of stealth. Using ancient Samurai stalking techniques developed over generations (like not carrying pockets full of loose change, whistling a happy tune or wearing day-glo colors), Ninjas can move silently and invisibly to strike at their prey!

    Their ability to blend into the darkness is undoubtedly the Ninjas' greatest asset, as we will now demonstrate. There are eight Ninjas hidden in the picture below. See if you can spot them (The answer's at the foot of this page.)

Because of their mysterious ways, a lot of legends have grown up around Ninjas and it's important to know what's true.

Answer

NINJAS – FACT FILE

Fact

- Ninjas always dress in black with scarves to cover their faces.
- They are masters of concealment, and darkness and shadow are their elements.
- They will pursue a victim until the assassination has been carried out, no matter how long this might take.
- They can last days without sleep or food.
- They attack when you're least expecting it.
- They are experts in using ancient Japanese weapons.
- Ninja's never eat baked beans (for obvious reasons).
- They are supremely proficient in unarmed combat and know twenty different ways to break your neck using just their ears or buttocks.
- You wouldn't want to meet one.

Fiction

- They're frightened of the dark.
- They can't stand the sight of blood.
- Ray Charles was once a Ninja.
- They won't attack you if you're asleep because it's not sporting.
- They listen to reason.
- They don't like heights.
- They crave pepperoni pizzas and announce their presence by shouting 'Cowabunga !'
- Their uniforms incorporate loads of tiny bright electric lights and a klaxon that plays 'Yankee Doodle' on the hour.
- 'Ninja' means, literally, 'Mars Bar'.

140

I SEE WHAT YOU MEAN. BUT WHAT'S THE BEST WAY TO DEFEAT THEM?

If you think there's a Ninja about, then the first thing to do is tempt (or taunt) him out of hiding. That way he loses his advantage and you can face him on equal terms. You can't tempt Ninjas out of places of concealment by obvious means – like, it's no use smacking your lips and saying, 'Mmmmm! I've got some delicious strawberry shortcake here and there's more than enough for one!' Use some real psychology. Say:

* 'Oh, what was that? Did I hear an illustrious ancestor just say, "Come out of hiding or face the wrath of unquiet spirits"?'
* 'Oh, look what's down here! A bottle of Johnny Walker Black Label.' (The thing the Japanese revere above all else – even whale cutlets.)
* 'Hands up all those who'd like to build a Death Railway!'
* 'Quick! There's a dolphin! Kill it!'

Being proud warriors steeped in centuries of tradition, Ninjas are very easily upset if insulted and can therefore be taunted out of the shadows by any of the following casual comments:

* 'I know *something else* that's silent and deadly – my farts.'
* 'Hiroshima. What a laugh, eh?'
* 'Ninjas sleep with the bedroom light on!'
* 'I bet you're hiding because you've got a really small dick.'
* 'Koi carp? What an ugly looking fish!'
* 'Come out, you turtle bastard!'
* 'Hirohito wore women's clothing!'
* 'More trade tariffs, eh? Scared of a little foreign competition, are we?'

OK, I GET THE PICTURE, BUT ISN'T THERE A NEW BREED OF NINJAS WHO ARE FAR MORE SUBTLE AND MODERN THAN THE TRADITIONAL NINJA?

All right, smartass, we were going to move on to that subject next anyway.

I BET YOU WEREN'T.

Yes, we were. It's in our book synopsis. Just ask the publishers.

I DON'T BELIEVE YOU. I BET YOU HADN'T EVEN THOUGHT OF IT UNTIL I MENTIONED IT.

Look, we know more about superheroes and supervillains than you could ever hope to. Now, do you want to want to know about the other type of Ninjas or not?

S'POSE SO.

Good. Then perhaps you'll shut it and let us get on before we run out of space.

●#HOLES.

What was that?

NOTHING.

Good. Just watch it, bud. Anyway, to continue, this new breed of Ninjas don't assassinate their victims by creeping up behind them and impaling them on something razor-sharp. Instead, they tend to rely on a more subtle and uniquely Japanese technique:

THE MODERN NINJA ASSASSINATION METHOD

The Japanese, inscrutable people that they are, have long since mastered the art of writing inscrutable and frankly incomprehensible instruction manuals in a strange form of pseudo-English.

A lot of electronic equipment used by superheroes is Japanese in origin, and it's been known for Ninjas to deliberately substitute the instructions for ones that are even more confusing – instructions that are so badly written that, at best, they will cripple the superhero's effectiveness and, at worst, even goad the superhero into having an apoplectic fit and dying. (Occasionally though, they get their assignments mixed up and these deadly instructions end up boxed with hi-fis, VCRs and cameras – as you probably already know to your cost...)

Anyway, this is the sort of thing you should be wary of:

TOIKYOTO Z-15 SUPER-BUDDY ™ MINI COMPUTER CRIME LAP-TOP ®

Much Important Read (High Voltage Death Doing)

Thank you friend of Toikyoto Corporation for such purchase of number 1 epoch-making technology machine. Crime fighting now you OK. Yes!

You able plot city roads link. Ready for action stations as large RAM capacity access you make. And exact locate. Time after every occasion meat grinder.

But instruct you special care for best look after operation. No break if this done allways. Also plenty raisin for screen!

1. Before using machinery memory to select output mode matrix. No done if you map area square 16 kilometres or plenty.
2. Button red is no turn delightful.
3. Modem link danger! Never interface direct to bison or risk inflammation!
4. Best uses possible if disk driving dump not symbolic of three. No microprocessor or Bob's-your-uncle (Divot Pin!).
5. You format expansion faciltate easy load green. Off.(XIK only Rodney!)
6. Jackplug for socketing direct to No shifting lock take for happiness.
7. Sleeper mode uppermost to be launched Catholic (No Torso farside guide).
8. Connecting to be.
9. Maximum potential by alighting 14.(NB. Loose Ocean no Kneecap or erupt!)
10 Danger is scraunching the marmoset!

EVIL MAGICIANS

It's particularly hard for superheroes to hunt down Evil Magicians because they're so easily confused with the thousands of legitimate, friendly magicians around the country – the type that entertain at cabarets, children's parties, weddings and bar mitzvahs.

So, to find and defeat Evil Magicians, you must be able to tell the difference.

MAGICIANS (evil)

EVIL MAGICIANS – FACT FILE

Fact

- They're not very nice.
- They absolutely hate doves and white rabbits.
- Many have sold their souls to Satan in exchange for immeasurable power.
- They know thousands of spells for all occasions.
- They can channel large amounts of energy through their magic wands.
- They're often over a thousand years old.

Fiction

- Their favorite trick is folding balloons into little doggies.
- They work cruise liners or resorts in the Catskills in the winter.
- When they drop something they make a witty ad lib like 'This trick takes   a lot of picking up.'
- They can be placated by offering them herrings.
- They're very welcome at children's parties.
- They get their tricks from *Magic for Beginners.*
- They have a dumb blonde assistant called Shirley, who dresses in sequins and waves her arms about a lot.
- They're all looking for the break that lets them turn pro.

Although most magicians dress alike, whether evil or just working to make an honest buck – in dark suit, top hat, white gloves and short black cape – you can usually detect a genuine Evil Magician by his name.

These are all genuine Evil Magicians:

* Dr Faustus
* The Ace of Wands
* The Voodoo Vixen
* The Vanishing Skull
* Sattana the Sinister Sorcerer
* Soggoth the Undying One
* Soth the Spellbinder
* Black Magic Master
* The Mad Magus
* The Warlock of Death
* Necromancer, the Evil One
* Wu-Chung the Merciless

...While these are definitely not:

* Old Mr Khadouri and his Pop-up Bunny Rabbit Delights
* Mr Magico and Zelda
* Frankie Houdini and his Disappearing Parrot
* Uncle Johnny and Dumpo the Flatulent Cat
* Grandpa Ashley and his Aquatic Three Ring Circus
* Witchipoo and Tomkin the Cat
* Mr Predicto and his Psychic Assistant, Darren
* Jay Presto!
* Smartie Artie's Conjuring Speciality Act
* The Great Marvo (with a prize for EVERY boy and girl!)
* Wizard Willie and his Balloon Folding Spectacular

Evil Magicians will also frequently give themselves away by the things they say:

Things Evil Magicians say:

– 'I summon the dark forces of Zoltar!'
– 'My power wand will unleash 200 kilotons of pure Satanic energy!'
– 'Die, Superhero trash!'
– 'By the arcane magic of Crystos, I cast you into the pit of Kylosis!'
– 'I summon thee, O restless spirits of the dead!'
– 'Stay back or the girl gets sawn in half!'
– 'AbracaDIE!'

Things Evil Magicians never say:

– 'Hey presto!'
– 'Before your very eyes...'
– 'Pick a card, any card.'
– 'Think of a number'
– 'Can I have a volunteer from the audience?'
– 'Abracadabra!'
– 'Open Sesame!'

HOW CAN I DEFEAT AN EVIL MAGICIAN?

Once you have ascertained that the magician in question is indeed evil, approach him with a large mirror secreted behind your back. The moment he unleashes his most potent spell at you, whip out the mirror and deflect it straight back at him! It's as simple as that!

IS IT?

Yes.

I'LL BET IT'S NOT. I'LL PROBABLY END UP SPENDING THE REST OF MY LIFE AS A TOAD.

We'd prove it to you, but sadly we've run out of space on this topic.

MAD PROFESSORS

EXACTLY WHAT IS A MAD PROFESSOR?

See the fact file opposite; it won't help you all that much – since all professors fit this description! It's far better to look at what someone who you suspect might be a mad scientist is busy inventing to gauge their mental state...

– Reversible sanitary napkins
– Toaster especially for slices of bread 8" thick
– A device that projects an image of Richard Gere on to your girlfriend's face as you make love
– Bowling alleys 6 feet long
– Male contraceptive pill that's 2% effective and is taken as a suppository
– Baseball bats made out of glass
– Baseballs made out of meringue
– Eau de Sealion parfum de toilette

MAD PROFESSORS – FACT FILE

Fact

- They've passed loads of exams and have letters after their names.
- They've never gone steady.
- They're always inventing things.
- Their deformed assistants are usually called Igor.
- They pulled the legs off spiders when they were kids.
- They laugh to themselves hysterically for no apparent reason.
- They understood the Quantum Theory when they were eight.
- They have loads of electronic equipment that goes 'beep'.
- They feel spurned and alienated by society.
- They were comic book fans when they were young.

Fiction

- They're perfectly sane.
- They're snappy dressers.
- Their laboratories are always left unlocked with a sign on the door saying, 'Come right in and have a good nose around'.
- They're always seen on the arm of a pretty girl at film premières.
- They won football scholarships to university.
- They're bright purple with two heads and tentacles.
- They really do care about their appearance.
- They lost their virginity (on average) at thirteen.

- Revolutionairy 9,000-calories-a-day diets
- Typewriters with the 'A' and 'S' keys tranposed
- Video cassettes containing fifteen seconds' worth of tape
- A new fruit that's a cross between a banana and a banana
- Colour film that's sensitive to the dark
- Rottweilers genetically altered to even more brain-dead than typical members of their species
- The Sinclair C5

OK. I GET THE PICTURE. MAD PROFESSORS ARE SCREWBALLS. HOW DO I STOP THEM?

Glad you asked that. The key to stopping mad professors is to make out that they're not *really* mad at all. This infuriates them like you wouldn't believe, as they try harder and harder to prove their insanity...

MAD PROFESSOR: Ha, ha, ha, Thunderman! I've got my finger on the button! One little push and California will plunge into the ocean!

SUPERHERO: (Holding arms outstretched and walking round in a circle) Whoo! I'm mad and I don't care what you do, chubby chops!

MAD PROFESSOR: You're not mad. *I'm mad*!

SUPERHERO: (Doing the twist) Not as mad as me, my fine feathered friend, my liddle chickadee! Banana, zim, zim, zim!

MAD PROFESSOR: Yes I am. I'm a mad professor!

SUPERHERO: (Sings) I-I-I-I-I-I-like you very much. I don't care. I'm madder than you'll ever be, Humphrey Bogart-Bottom!

MAD PROFESSOR: (Getting angrier) You can't be! I'm the mad one. That's why I'm destroying California.

SUPERHERO: (Doing a moonwalk) You're not even a tiny bit mad. Hubba, hubba, hubba!

MAD PROFESSOR: Of course I'm mad. I'm stark raving mad! I'm going to cause a geological catastrophe and drown millions of innocent victims! If that's not *mad*, what is?

SUPERHERO: (Doing a handstand) So what?

MAD PROFESSOR: I don't care how many people I kill – because I'm *mad*! In fact, I'm as *mad* as a March hare!

SUPERHERO: Well, I'm round the bend! I'm one sandwich short of a picnic! I'm off my rocker! I'm sappy! I'm scatty! I'm screwy! I'm a dumdum! I'm batty! I'm a crackpot! I'm crazy as a coot! I'm bananas! I'm kooky! I'm loco! I'm out of my head! There's nobody home! I'm bonzo! I'm a few cards short of a full deck! I'm cockamamie! I'm off my noodle! I'm out to lunch! I'm off my trolley! I'm meshugah! I'm seriously bonkers! I'm a loony-tune! I'm daffy! I'm cuckoo! I'm dickbrained! I'm half-baked! I'm mental! I'm a headcase! I'm squirrel munchies! I'm wacko! I'm a certified ding-a-ling! I'm a full-mooner! I'm kooky! I'm down for a Section Eight!

MAD PROFESSOR: OK ,wise guy, you may be mad, but I bet I've done *madder* things than you could ever have dreamed of! I once slammed my fingers in a door just for a bet!

148

SUPERHERO: So? I do that every morning when I get up – just for fun!

MAD PROFESSOR: Well, I purposely stabbed a ballpoint in my eye to celebrate Washington's birthday!

SUPERHERO: (Punching himself in the face) Well ... (oooh!) ... I've ... done (ouch!) ... that ... four ... times ... this .. (oof!) ... week!

MAD PROFESSOR: What about the time I shattered both my kneecaps with a baseball bat for no apparent reason?

SUPERHERO: Seen it. Done it. Been there.

MAD PROFESSOR: Or stuck my fingers in a food processor?

SUPERHERO: Yesterday's news, pookie-pookie.

MAD PROFESSOR: (Getting more frustrated) Hand in a bonfire?

SUPERHERO: Passé.

MAD PROFESSOR: Foot under a pneumatic jackhammer?

SUPERHERO: (Frantically playing with himself) Yawn!

MAD PROFESSOR: OK, big shot. What have you done that's so brilliantly mad?

SUPERHERO: (Holding both hands up to his head with fingers apart, doing an impression of an elk) I stuck a neutron grenade up my ass and set it off! Pow! *Sphincter tartare!*

MAD PROFESSOR: Oh? Whoopie sho! That's sooooo bigshot mad!

SUPERHERO: I poured concentrated acid down my pants through a funnel.

MAD PROFESSOR: Ooooh! I'm sooo jealous! That's not mad – it's feeb city!

SUPERHERO: Mad? Of course it's mad. Do you think pouring acid all over your genitals is a rational act? Do you think a sane man would try to dissolve his penis because he felt like it? You don't know what 'mad' is. You're a fake, *El Fraudo!*

MAD PROFESSOR: (Trying to pull off both his ears) Oh, yeah?

SUPERHERO: (Flapping his arms like a bird) Yeah!

MAD PROFESSOR: OK, Mr Wise Guy. How's this for 'mad'? HA! HA! HA! (Takes a ray gun out of his inside coat pocket, puts the barrel in his mouth and pulls the trigger) – **ZZZTTT!!**

SUPERHERO: You were right – you were *f@#$ing mad*....

MAN-DROIDS

WHAT THE HELL ARE 'MAN-DROIDS'?

Pardon me?

YOU HEARD ME. I SAID WHAT ARE 'MAN-DROIDS?'

...

YOU DON'T KNOW, DO YOU?

Yes, we do.

NO, YOU DON'T. YOU'RE JUST PLAYING FOR TIME SO YOU CAN REACH THE BOTTOM OF THE PAGE AND THEN SAY SOMETHING LIKE, 'OH DEAR, WE SEEM TO HAVE RUN OUT OF SPACE,' THEN GO ON TO SOMETHING YOU MIGHT ACTUALLY KNOW ABOUT.

No, we're not.

OK. SO WHAT ARE 'MAN-DROIDS' THEN?

Did you say 'Androids'?

LOOK, WISEGUYS. IF YOU DON'T TELL ME WHAT 'MAN-DROIDS' ARE, I'M GOING TO TELL ALL MY BUDDIES THAT I MET YOU AND YOU'RE BOTH REAL FAGGOTY AND TRIED TO TOUCH ME UP WHEN I ASKED FOR YOUR AUTOGRAPHS!

You wouldn't do that ... *would you*?

TRY ME.

A 'Man-Droid' is basically someone who wears a protective armor-plated electronic battle suit. These usually contain an onboard computer, integral

oxygen supply and provide protection against severe heat and cold, electric shocks, poisonous chemicals and nasty things like that.

Typically, loads of gadgets like jet thrusters, X-ray scanners, laser torches, acoustic pick-ups, filtration units and directional radar are built in, making the wearer a self-contained fighting unit, sealed against the environment and virtually impregnable.

IF THEY'RE ARMOR-PLATED AND SEALED UP, HOW CAN THEY BE DEFEATED?

Well, the fact that they're sealed up is the one chink in their armor, so to speak. Man-Droids count on only being locked in their armor for relatively short periods of time so there is no in-built provision for ... going to the john.

This means that if you can make Man-Droids want to take a leak, they'll feel very uncomfortable. Holding their groin and flying cross-legged will severely hamper their fighting abilities – as will actually pissing in their suits and short-circuiting all the vital electronic equipment.

AHA! I SEE NOW! SO, HOW CAN I MAKE MAN-DROIDS PISS THEMSELVES?

- Creep up behind them and whisper 'Psss-swsss-swsss-swsss-swsss' into their suit's acoustic pick-ups
- Fight them over Niagara Falls
- Leave a tap dripping back at the Crimecave and broadcast the sound over your accessory belt transceiver
- Make them chase you along the entire length of the Mississippi
- 'Accidentally' smash the tops off several fire hydrants in the course of a battle
- Wear a toilet seat around your neck and say it's part of your costume
- Complement your normal Cyclotronic Phaser Gun with a water pistol
- Play toilet flushing sound effects from your Crimemobile loud speakers.
- Start singing 'Drip, drip, drip little April Showers', 'Rainy Night in Georgia' or 'Three Coins in a Fountain'
- Turn up with another superhero like Hydro-Master who's brought with him his superpet – a trained blue whale named Spouter
- Paint a picture of a giant watering can on the front of your costume
- Tell them they've been indicted for tax fraud and that at that very moment the Internal Revenue Service are going through their accounts with a fine-tooth comb.

MASTERS OF EVIL

The most evil supervillains think of themselves as Masters of Evil and their goal is *always* world domination.

MASTERS OF EVIL – FACT FILE

FACT

- They're mentally unbalanced.
- They steal, kill and take over things they're not supposed to.
- They fight superheroes.
- They pose a substantial threat to the future of mankind.
- They will betray their fellow supervillains to save their own skins.
- They drop nuclear devices on to whale breeding colonies just for the heck of it.
- Masters of Evil develop nasty death-dealing devices like the fabled (and dreaded) Whang-Manglotron.
- They boast about their plans for world domination in order to give superheroes a chance to escape.

FICTION

- Masters of Evil say 'please' and 'thank you'.
- They send Christmas cards.
- They remember their mother's birthday.
- They wash their hands after using the toilet.
- They show everyone their Scout badges.
- They grow their own root vegetables.
- They carry a bar of chocolate around with them in case they get peckish.
- They patronize contemporary dance theatre.
- They become 'Parents-by-Post'.
- They signal before making a turn.

They invariably attempt to hold the world to ransom. Some threats you must respond to immediately. Others it's safe to ignore (well, they are mentally unbalanced...)

153

HOW DO I DEFEAT A MASTER OF EVIL?

When you go into battle against any supervillain, whether a Master of Evil or not, it's vitally important to do it *in style*, appearing casual and unperturbed by making witty little quips.

It's quite easy, really. There are two main rules to remember:

RULE 1.

A witty quip contains two elements: (a) a phrase to signify that your opponent has been, or is about to be, defeated; (b) his name. The important thing to remember, and a point where a lot of Superheroes go wrong, is that there has to be a pun linking the two.

For example, it's no good saying something like 'It's the end of the road for you, Doctor Maelstrom!' In this example there is nothing that links the first part of the phrase with the enemy you are fighting, and instead of being a witty quip, this becomes a f@#$ing stupid quip.

RULE 2.

The other important point to note is that witty quips should only be used when you're positive the battle is almost won and you're about to deliver the *coup de grâce*. It's no good making a witty quip like 'That just about wraps it up for you, Paper Man!' right at the beginning of the fight and then getting severely injured.

So, armed with this advice, here are some examples of witty quips.

- 💡 It's the end of the line for you, Locomotive Lad!
- 💡 It's curtains for you, Fabric Master!
- 💡 I'd call that checkmate, Grand Master!
- 💡 It's the end of the road for you, Highwayman!
- 💡 It's the last dance, Waltzer!
- 💡 That just about ties it up for you, Rope Master!
- 💡 That's the final whistle, Music Man!
- 💡 Your race is run, Speed Master!
- 💡 That just about winds it up, Doctor Tick-Tock!
- 💡 Your bubble has burst, Baron Soap!
- 💡 It's the final bell, Chime Master!
- 💡 It's your last roundup, Cattle Man!
- 💡 That's the final chapter, Book Master!
- 💡 It's bedtime for you, Doctor Nightmare!
- 💡 *Au revoir*, Bad Penny!
- 💡 You're fø#$ed, Reproductive Man!
- 💡 You're herringed, Doc Surreal!
- 💡 Time to hog-tie you, Porker-King!
- 💡 It's all over now, Baron Diversity!
- 💡 Time to call it a day, Twenty-Four-Hour Man
- 💡 Say good night, Gracie!

FIGHTING SUPERVILLAINS IS RISKY, ISN'T IT? YOU'VE BEEN HOLDING BACK...

Perhaps now's the time for straight talking. There may come a time in the career of every superhero when he's faced with *certain death*. It's nothing to be ashamed of – as long as you know how to behave properly when the time comes.

Good things to do in the face of certain death
- Spit
- Laugh
- Salute your enemy
- Sing 'The Star-Spangled Banner' or 'America The Beautiful' proudly and defiantly
- Detonate the small nuclear device in your accessory belt to take your enemy with you!
- Ask for one final phone call and, by tapping in a certain combination of keys, summon the Crimemobile by remote control to race you away!
- Produce your concealed escape device
- Run as fast as you can
- Summon the other members of your Superteam by means of your miniature wrist signaling device
- Tell your enemy that the other members of your Superteam know exactly where you are and that if you fail to return, the consequences won't be worth thinking about
- Ask for a last request and opt for sex with Cher (or someone who looks quite like her)
- Talk your foe into believing that he's being double-crossed by other members of his gang

Bad things to do in the face of certain death
- Die
- Sh.. yourself
- Call for your mommy
- Beg
- Throw your Boy Wonder into the line of fire and take off
- Find out you don't believe in God after all
- Shout, 'Do your worst and do it slow!'
- Take off all your clothes and offer your foe your body
- Faint
- Find out you've left your concealed escape device back in the Crimecave
- Sob uncontrollably
- Discover the batteries in your miniature wrist signaling device have gone flat
- Tell your enemy that you don't belong to a Superteam, that no one knows where you are, and that all the other Superheroes hate you anyway because of your stretching powers.
- Ask for a last request – and opt for a God almighty kick in the nuts
- Tell your enemy that there's a $3,000,000 reward on your head, offered by Doctor Destructo

APPENDIX ONE:
JOINING A SUPERTEAM

HUBBA! HUBBA! TIFFANY, NAKED AND RUNNING THROUGH THIS CORNFIELD ... AND I'M NAKED TOO AND I'VE GOT THIS GIANT TIN OF PEACHES IN SYRUP AND A BIG STICK AND...

Hey, whoever's thinking that out there, can they please stop it! The subject of this appendix is 'Joining a Superteam', not scuzzy adolescent male fantasies.

SORRY. I DIDN'T REALIZE WE'D STARTED AGAIN.

Well, we have, so pay attention. In the last ten years the number of active superteams in the world has more than quadrupled!

Some of the larger superteams have now opened branches throughout America so that, no matter where you live, you're within easy reach of a group of costumed crimefighters.

Of course, having so much choice can be confusing. Should you just go out and join the nearest team because it's convenient, or should you be more selective? We asked superheroes for their opinions...

'Be very careful who you join, that's my advice! My leader was an idiot. I was treated like dirt, half of our equipment didn't work properly, morale was at rock-bottom and drug abuse was rife! Of course, then it suddenly dawned on me – I'd joined the US Army by mistake'
— The Hooded Arrow, Atlantic City, NJ

'Yeah, be careful. I joined the first costumed group I came across. Turned out to be the Ku Klux Klan (which is 'specially embarrassing for me 'cos I'm black inside this armor!)'
— The Steel Mandroid, Montgomery, AL

'Be careful of any groups charging you to join. Like asking for all your worldly goods, assets, properties, car, stocks and bonds and savings. You're probably on the verge of joining the Moonies!'
— Mightyman, New York, NY

'I got the forms all switched round at home. I went to my first meeting only to find I'd joined the Brownies ... and my seven-year-old became a member of the International Crimebusting Squad.
She's now their mascot ... and I'm working towards my "Little Helper" badge'
— Powerlance, Utica, NY

So, before you consider joining any superteam, stop and ask yourself a few, simple questions.

1) DO YOU LIKE THE SOUND OF THE SUPERTEAM?

Names of superteams are important because they tell you a lot about the kind of group you're about to join. Make sure you find out *exactly* what the intitials of your superteam stand for before you commit yourself.

For example, FIST might sound like a real rugged outfit to hang out with, but it could stand for *Fairies Into Sadistic Tendencies*, or the *Flatulent & Incontinent Superheroes Team*, or even *Fe#%ing Idiotic Superhero Turtles.*

Make certain that your superteam has at least one of these words in its name:

Justice	Challengers	All-Stars	Titanic
Avenging	Two-fisted	Protectors	Crusaders
Winners	Strikeforce	Almighty	Sentinels
Invincible	Defenders	Guardians	Glorious
American	Liberty	Fantastic	Remarkable
Dynamite	Heroic	Annihilators	Nymphomaniacs

Words to watch out for in a superteam's name might include:

Doom	Lepers	Superpets	Scaredy-Cats
Suicide	Underdogs	Buggery	Spazmo
Pacifists	No-hopers	Wombats	Decrepit
Longshots	Inferior	Morons	Ugly
Masochists	Pariahs	Evangelists	Number Two's
Losers	Outcasts	Retreaters	Queer
Cream puffs	Sh@ Heels	Ticklers	Klutz
Bizarre	Marxist-Leninists	Geekoids	Crap

Have they made a mistake altogether with their name? For example, at first thought 'The Trojans' might sound like a great name for a rough, tough superteam, but...

2) DOES THE SUPERTEAM HAVE THE KIND OF MEMBERS YOU WANT TO BE ASSOCIATED WITH ?

Do any key team members rely on power over sandwiches to fight crime, for example, or powers which are limited to communicating with earthworms? Is anyone on the team roster called Flatulence Man or Jism King? Remember, you will be cooped up in the team Crimecave or on board the team satellite with these people!

You will also have to fight alongside these superheroes, and your life may well depend on their actions. Could you trust your life to anyone called Peanut Butter Master, for example, or expect a man with power over his own pubic hair to save you from a death trap?

Also – and perhaps most important of all – are any members called anything like Psycho, Schitzoman or Turncoat?

Inspect the team roster thoroughly before committing yourself.

3) DO THEY FIGHT THE TYPE OF SUPERVILLAINS YOU WANT TO TACKLE?

Every superteam has its own regular rogues' gallery of arch villains with whom they regularly clash. Find out who they are. Any superteam whose rogues' gallery includes 'Castration Squad' should be avoided.

4) WHAT IS DAY-TO-DAY LIFE IN THE TEAM LIKE?

Take a look at the team noticeboard to see what's happening.
A good team to join might display:

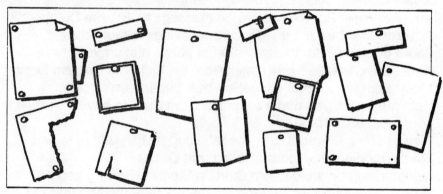

1. Letter of thanks on United Nations stationery
2. Duty roster for assignments in Paris, Milan and Hong Kong
3. Newsclipping about the Superteam saving the world (again)
4. Announcement of forthcoming visit from the President
5. Certificate awarding the team the freedom of the planet Neptune
6. List of new codes for operating worldwide telepod network
7. Invitation to address Congress on the 'Evil Mutoids' question
8. $20 bill with a note saying that this was found on the floor of the Transmitter Room
9. Photograph torn from a space technology magazine
10. The cover of that Superteam's latest comic
11. Begging letter from the Bangles' management for a photo opportunity
12. Letter confirming a sponsorship deal with a large cola manufacturer

13. 'Superhero of the Year' rules and entry form
14. Letter from ex-Superteam member thanking colleagues for their generous leaving present
15. Note from Superteam leader congratulating all members on their efforts in tracking down and defeating a Cyborg menace
16. Thank-you card from The Hammerhead for the flowers he received following his recent minor hernia operation
17. Notice that the gymnasium will be shut for a week due to complete refurbishment
18. Note giving details of future courses in martial arts, advanced laser weaponry and crime detection techniques

A bad team to join might display:

1. Letter from local residents asking them to keep the noise down
2. Washing-up rota
3. Newsclipping about the arrest of a Superteam member for exposing himself in K-Mart
4. Local Pizza Hut takeaway menu
5. Card that says 'Relaxed unhurried massage by Buxom Dominatrix'
6. Advertisement from a team member selling his moped
7. Photo of pig with 'our leader' written above it in crayon
8. Note saying that $53 was stolen from the locker of Captain Eagle
9. Letter from a publisher cancelling that Superteam's comic
10. Note reminding you that it's against team rules to have a woman in your room after 10.30
11. Picture of Paula Abdul with obscene suggestion added in biro
12. Bill demanding nine months' back rent on HQ
13. Incriminating polaroids from Captain Eternal's leaving party
14. Note from Superteam leader to all members reminding them to flush the toilet after use
15. Thank-you cards from the widows of Mr Invincible and Captain Strong for the wreaths they received following their husbands' tragic deaths
16. Notice that the pool and gynasium will be shut indefinitely due to yeast infection
17. Empty packet of Frit-O-Lays unaccountably pinned to board

5) DO THEY HAVE THE VERY LATEST TECHNOLOGY?

♀ Can you reach superteam HQ by your own teleportation pod, or do you have to hitch? (This can be a real problem, especially when the headquarters are on board a satellite in earth orbit).

♀ Are you issued with personal communicator rings to talk to other team members – or will you have to fall back on shouting and making furious arm gestures in the heat of combat?

♀ Is there a team jet – or just a minibus with your team name painted on the side?

♀ Can you monitor distress calls from around the world on your own state-of-the-art computer monitoring system – or do you have to rely on hearsay?

♀ Is your team HQ packed with automatic defense systems – or does Mr Midnight bring in his Rottweiler?

♀ Is there a computerized Battle Room where you can hone your strategies against a variety of simulated assaults – or just a bare wall where you can shadowbox if you feel like it?

♀ Is there a portal to the Negative Space/Time Continuum in the lab – or just a backdoor you use to take out the trash?

♀ Do you have a team time machine which enables you to battle menaces from the future – or do you just have to be patient and wait?

♀ Is the HQ fitted with a fully equipped medical lab to treat casualties – or do you rely entirely on a few elastoplasts and a bottle of antiseptic lotion hidden away in a cupboard somewhere?

6) DO YOU AGREE WITH THE AIMS OF THE SUPERTEAM?

Not all superteams are founded with the express purpose of fighting crime. Many of those who set up their own superteam have their own *very personal* (and consequently incomprehensible) reasons for doing so. Watch out for teams sworn to:

☆ Protect jams and jellies of all flavors

☆ Promote the eating of cheese

☆ Fight anything beginning with the letter P

☆ Guard the sovereignty of Liechtenstein

☆ Save the human race from nylon

☆ Get more *Star Trek* re-runs on TV

☆ Spread the Mormon gospel

☆ Stop people eating defenseless radishes

☆ Prevent Andy Williams from taking over the known universe

☆ Defend anything beginning with the letter R

☆ Promote harmonious sexual relations between man and marsupial

☆ Persuade Dr Ruth to pose naked for *Playboy*

☆ Recreate the Battle of Gettysburg on the first Sunday of every month

☆ Preserve the memory of Roy Rogers and Trigger

☆ Prove that the Lost City of Atlantis really did exist – where Des Moines is today.

7) IS THERE A TEAM BATTLE SONG?

Do you really want to go into battle singing

'We are mean and we are butch
We are here to kick some tush!...'
(Battle Team X)

Or

'We are the superheroes
De Dum De Dum De Dum
De Da De Da De Da'
(Supersquad)

Or

'We're proud to be in the Liberty Team
(YODEL-ODEL-ODEL-ODEL-OH-OH-OH!)
We fight crime wherever it's seen
(YODEL-ODEL-ODEL-ODEL-OH!)
(YODEL-OH-OH-OH!)
(YODEL-OH-OH-OH)
(YODEL-OH-OH-OH!)
(YODEL-OH-OH-OH)
(YODEL-ODEL-ODEL-ODEL-OHHHHH!!!)'

(The Liberty Team)

Or even...

'Yow! Check it out, supersucka!
Ch-ch-ch-eck! Ch-ch-ch-check!
I'm a righteous hero
An' you're a zero

162

You be Rome an' I be Nero!
You're a woosey, gonna be a doozy!
Don't mean spit if you're packing an Uzi...
'Cause I'll zap ya, gonna whap ya,
With my superpowers!
Gonna chill ya, gonna ill ya –
You be pushin' up flowers!
'Cause I'm it, Jack. Ain't no other
Bought a condo for my mother.
An' your girl wants me, an' she'll be free
When I put an end to your robbin' spree!'

(Power Posse – Mastermix Jack 7" version)

No. We didn't think so.

Most teams are now vaguely embarrassed about their team songs, especially those originally influenced by Abba and the Partridge Family, and have made them entirely optional. Clarify the point before you commit yourself!

8) OVERALL, IS THE TEAM A 'GOOD' TEAM TO JOIN?

The golden rule is to avoid joining any team which sounds particularly dangerous ... or stupid.

DANGEROUS SUPERTEAMS

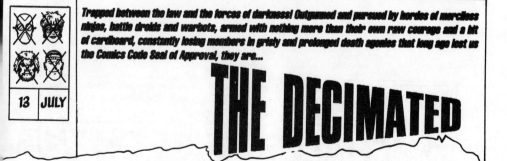

Trapped between the law and the forces of darkness! Outgunned and pursued by hordes of merciless ninjas, battle droids and warbots, armed with nothing more than their own raw courage and a bit of cardboard, constantly losing members in grisly and prolonged death agonies that long ago lost us the Comics Code Seal of Approval, they are...

THE DECIMATED

13 JULY

No odds are too great for them! No task too perilous! If the odds are actually in their favor, they deliberately hamper themselves! So was the oath they swore, the day they became...

CHALLENGERS OF THE

COMICS CODE: "DEFINITELY IMPOSSIBLE!"

IMPOSSIBLE

19 JAN

They sneer at danger! They laugh in the face of death! They have no interest at all in their own personal safety! They are...

THE CRETINS

12 AUG

STUPID SUPERTEAMS

When Danger threatens, they might be there. When evil strikes, there's always the possibility they might do something about it. For they are...

THE UNRELIABLES

19 JAN

THEY OPERATE IN STRICT SECRECY, DOING THE JOB NOBODY ELSE WANTS TO HANDLE. NOBODY ASKS THEM HOW THEY DO IT. THE LESS YOU KNOW ABOUT THEM, THE BETTER. YOU'LL PROBABLY BE SICK BEFORE PAGE 7. THEY ARE...

CHALLENGERS OF THE SEPTIC

84 AUG

217 DEC

Specky, Blob, Titch, Pee-Wee, Wiggly and Proto – Names carved in the Superheroes' Hall of Fame! Wherever evil or injustice exists on a unicellular level, that's where you'll find them! They are...

THE LEGION OF AMOEBAS

48 OCT

Paddler, Backlash, Slapmaster, 'English' Rose, Buttox, King Tush and The Beatmaster – seven superheroes who have joined together to right the wrongs of the universe ... by capturing supervillains and giving them a sound spanking!
– It doesn't work, but they all have a great time trying! They are the...

ALL STAR SPANKING SQUAD

31 MAY

Whenever danger calls – they're not there! Wherever villainy raises its ugly head – that's where you're exceptionally unlikely to find them! Hell, they don't even send Christmas cards, because they are....

THE DEAD

52 MAR

Dedicated to fighting crime by lowering their pants and friskily wiggling their buttocks at the world's most powerful supervillains! They are....

HINDQUARTER ACTION LIKE YOU'VE NEVER SEEN IT BEFORE!

THE MOONIES

I'VE HEARD OF A SUPERTEAM CALLED SUPERHEROES ANONYMOUS. ARE THEY A GOOD TEAM TO JOIN?

Superheroes Anonymous is not a superteam at all – it's an organization especially set up to help those unfortunates who have become addicted to the role of a superhero and are no longer able to lead a normal life.

Members are encouraged to attend regular meetings and to share their experiences with fellow members.

We have obtained part of a highly secret transcript from one of these closed meetings...

CAPTAIN COURAGEOUS: My name is Captain Courageous and I've been ... a superhero for five years now. I thought I could keep it separate from my normal life, but gradually it began to take over.

Just stupid little things at first, like turning to my wife after making love and saying, 'No need to thank me, ma'am: I'm just doing my job' – before jumping out the window and running down the street stark naked.

Then I began to think and talk like a superhero all the time. Soon, I found that I couldn't pass a phone booth without rushing inside and pulling my pants down – whether the booth was empty or not.

But, worst of all, I was compelled to solve every problem with my fists – domestic arguments, two Jehovah's Witnesses who wouldn't go away, even awkward crossword puzzles. I realized then that I had a *problem* and, of course, tried to settle it in true superhero fashion – I punched myself half way across the Appalachians before I realized what I was doing!

So, now I've decided to *do something* to sort out my life! I'm determined to... Oh, is that an almost imperceptible distress call I can hear? Excuse me!

(Chairs fly everywhere as all the superheroes rush from the hall, bursting through doors, windows, walls and the ceiling, de-materializing, teleporting, bursting into flame, shrinking down and straddling flying ants, converting themselves into beams of light or unleashing their magic dopplegangers)

(PAUSE)

(Captain Courageous returns to the hall)

CAPTAIN COURAGEOUS: Er ... false alarm ... Sorry. Hello? Hello? Anyone?

APPENDIX TWO:
SUPERPETS

If you can't have a Boy Wonder, (perhaps because of a previous court ruling, for example), then the next best thing may well be a superpet.

If you decide to turn your own trusty pet *Ol' Shep* into a superpet, be prepared for some very real changes in your relationship. It won't be any use going to the backdoor and calling him in for his Rumpy-Chunks any more. He won't be able to hear you because he's busy sniffing around Neptune. You'll have to be prepared for armored contingents of the National Guard delivering your mail, summoning him with a dog whistle the size of the Mount Palomar telescope, taking him for walks securely tethered with twelve steel ship's cables, stroking him with a baseball bat, tickling his tummy with a combine harvester – and using a lead-lined pooper-scooper to prevent a major environmental catastrophe.

And *Tiddles*, being the independent little wanderer that he is, could cause even more problems. He could cause millions of dollars' worth of damage just prowling the backyards of the neighborhood (which, to a supercat, can include most of the Eastern Seaboard) and a night on the tiles might prove even worse! His super-sprainting might even cause a panic the like of which hasn't been seen since Three Mile Island!

But the biggest drawback by far of turning beloved pets into superpets is that you're much more likely to flash-fry, melt, bisect, break, eviscerate, dice, dissolve, electrocute, squash, squish or disintegrate them in the process, rather than imbuing them with superpowers!

Best to go to your nearest pet store or zoo and see what they can let you have (don't tell them you're planning to wire the animal up to the mains and then pour chemicals over it – remember, they haven't read this book and so won't understand that you have a legitimate reason for your behavior!)

WHAT TYPE OF ANIMAL MAKES FOR THE BEST SUPERPET?

♀ Pit bull terriers (fast and ferocious!)

♀ Blue whales (an aqua-pal supreme!)

♀ Lions (look great at superteam meetings!)

♀ Moose (everyone remembers who you are!)

♀ Rhinoceroses (able to stand up to the crushing G-Force on Jupiter!)

I'VE GOT A DACHSHUND. WHAT ABOUT THAT?

What about that? Forget it if you want anyone to continue buying your comic! And while you're at it, forget...

☞ Skunks (you don't want one)

☞ Giant Pandas (too hard to recruit)

☞ Koala Bears (lazy little bastards!)

☞ Diplodocus (totally extinct)

☞ Penguins (they're all stupid, waddling asses)

☞ Ocelots (what for?)

☞ Three-Toed Sloths (only useful on hanging-upside-down missions)

HOW CAN I TURN MY ANIMAL INTO A SUPERPET?

As we've said, you can wire them up to the mains and then pour a series of experimental chemicals over them until you succeed in superpowering your pet – or until you need another one.

On the other hand, you can just let them roam freely for a few days. Animals, little scamps that they are, are always getting into trouble and may well end up *giving themselves* superpowers by...

☆ Pissing on the third rail after rolling in experimental chemicals

☆ Running to fetch a stick and instead retrieving an atomic device by mistake

☆ Chasing a truck that's transporting a crashed UFO to New Mexico for examination

☆ Having their fur groomed by a brush that comes from a parallel universe

☆ Biting the leg of a mailman who, unknowingly, has the latent genetic structure of a mutant

☆ Eating pet food that's been contaminated with neutron particles

☆ Being bitten by another radioactive pet

☆ Running on an exercise treadmill so fast that it reaches the specific vibration needed to achieve inter-dimensional travel

☆ (Parrots only) Trying to say 'Polly wants a cracker' but accidentally squawking the forgotten ancient magic word of the Lost Race of Xerxe that transforms them into a superpet

☆ Trying to hide a bone and digging up buried toxic waste

☆ Wearing a flea collar that attracts a Power Beam sent from the planet Argon

HEY, I'VE DONE IT! PET #141 IS A SUPERPET!

Congratulations! You now own potentially the most dangerous thing on the planet!

WHAT????

Once you've got your superpet, you have to train it to assist you in crimefighting. Left to their natural instincts, Superpets will carry on doing the things that they've done for thousands of years, like crapping, getting horny at the most inappropriate times and wanting their bellies tickled.

They won't be used to disarming a supervillain or gaining control of a renegade nuclear missile. That's where obedience classes come in. It's absolutely *vital* that your superpet recognizes and understands certain key commands:

GOOD COMMANDS TO TEACH YOUR SUPERPET

☞ 'Heel!'

☞ 'Play dead!'

☞ 'Fetch!'

☞ 'Fly!'

☞ 'Dematerialize!'

☞ 'Mutilate savagely!'

☞ 'Disarm!'

☞ 'Go get me my accessory belt that I left in the Crimecave!'

☞ 'Trail!'

☞ 'Overpower!'

☞ 'Defuse!'

☞ 'Arrest!'

☞ 'Deflect!'

☞ 'Call a doctor. Now!'

BAD COMMANDS TO TEACH YOUR SUPERPET

☆ 'Die!'

☆ 'Explode!'

☆ 'Scratch your balls!'

☆ 'Scratch my balls!'

☆ 'Rub yourself against my leg until I'm hot 'n' ready for it!'

☆ 'Sh@ on my head!'

☆ 'Barf!'

☆ 'Act like you don't have any superpowers at all!'

☆ 'Surrender!'

☆ 'Join forces with my opponent and defeat me!'

☆ 'Run away!'

☆ 'Bite my bottom!'

SHOULD I LET MY SUPERPET JOIN THE LEAGUE OF SUPERPETS?

That's an entirely academic question – because the League of Superpets no longer exists!

Oh, it seemed like a good idea at the time – a crimefighting team of superpets acting independently of their owners! Established by Super-Fifi, a French Poodle and Wonder-Simon, a silver-backed gorilla, the League somehow managed to base itself in a space station in a geosynchronous orbit high above the Earth.

Unfortunately, without guidance or commands from their masters the pets instantly reverted to their baser animal instincts and either ran amok or ate each other. Amazingly, the League managed to last for six weeks – before the satellite mysteriously blew up and plunged back to Earth in flames.

In its time, the League was responsible for preventing absolutely no crimes whatsoever.

This is how the League of Superpets saw itself:

Unfortunately, this is what it was like in reality:

171

HEY, WHY IS THIS LAST PAGE BLANK? I BET IT'S BECAUSE YOU'VE RUN OUT OF MATERIAL.

That's where you're wrong, pal! In fact our Psychotronic Helmet™ has abruptly broken down and we can't read your thoughts any more.

BUT YOU'VE JUST READ MY LAST ONE . . .

No we didn't.

OH YES YOU DID!

Er . . . what was that about a herring. . . (crackle). . . (crackle) . . .

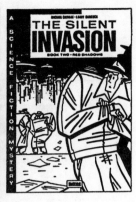

In a take-off of the Invasion of the Body Snatchers and The Day the Earth Stood Still, this four-volume story follows Matt Sinkage, a reporter in the Fifties, who's sure aliens are taking over people's bodies and our society. Others aren't so sure … Mixes humor and an involving suspenseful yarn.

Each: 80 pp., 8¼x11¾, B&W, color cover, trade pb:
Vol. 1: "Secret Affairs," $8.95
Vol. 2: "Red Shadows," $8.95
Vol. 3: "Tarnished Dreams," $9.95
Vol. 4: "The Great Fear," $9.95
Limited signed hardcover editions: $35 each
The complete set of signed hardcovers: $99

SUBURBAN NIGHTMARES

Cherkas ● Hancock ● Van Bruggen

The Fifties—a time of mindless happiness masking fear. Fear of the bomb, fear of commies, fear of being different. Cherkas and Hancock, authors of the critically acclaimed Silent Invasion, along with Van Bruggen, spin tales of special irony in light of the present vertiginous disintegration of communism.

8x11, 112 pp., B&W, color cover, trade pb: $10.95

Limited signed hardcover, numbered to 200, gold stamped: $39.50

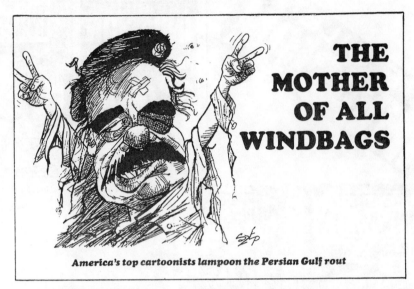

THE MOTHER OF ALL WINDBAGS

America's top cartoonists lampoon the Persian Gulf rout

Leading American cartoonists lampoon what became one of the more absurd events in human history. 60 cartoons by such nationally recognized names as Paul Szep, Tony Auth and Bill Mauldin. Get your souvenir book!
8½x5½, 64 pp., B&W, color cover, trade pb.: $5.95